# THE DECISION FORTRESS

## CONSTRUCTING UNSHAKEABLE LEADERSHIP, ONE DECISION AT A TIME

JUSTIN WILSON

Christian Leadership

*To my wife, who loves me enough to speak the hard truth and to my accountability group, who refuses to let me lower the standard.*

*I would not be the man I am today without you.*

# THE MAP IS GONE

You are doing everything right. You read your Bible. You tithe. You serve. You pray. Then the crisis hits.

Maybe it's the text message at 10:00 PM that threatens your marriage. Maybe it's the client canceling the contract that keeps your lights on. Maybe it's the moral dilemma where the profitable choice and the honest choice are two different things.

You freeze. You panic. You run to God and beg for a sign. You want a burning bush. You want a wet fleece. You want a notification on your phone that says, *"Turn Left Here to Save Your Career"*.

You want a Map, but the heavens are silent. The only thing you hear is the hum of the air conditioner and the silence is terrifying. It feels like abandonment. It feels like you've walked off the edge of the map and God has left the room.

**You are wrong. The silence is not a punishment. It is a promotion.**

∾

## The Junior vs. The Senior Engineer

I am a Chief Technology Officer (CTO). I have spent 18 years building engineering teams. In my world, there is a massive difference between a Junior Engineer and a Senior Engineer.

When I hire a **Junior Engineer**, I hold their hand. I give them a specific ticket. I tell them exactly what code to write. I micromanage them because they don't know the system yet. If they get stuck, I jump in immediately to help. They need a Map.

Now, look at the **Senior Engineer**. I do not give them a ticket; I give them a problem. *"The database is too slow. Please take a look at it."* I don't tell them how. I don't stand over their shoulder. I leave the room. Why? **Because I trust them.**

I trust that they know the architecture. I trust that they have internalized the principles of the business. I trust them to make a thousand micro-decisions without my constant input.

∾

### God is transitioning you from a Junior Engineer to a Senior Leader.

In the early days of your faith, God gave you constant feedback. The perfect song on the radio. The timely text from a friend. He handed you a Map because you were a child, but God isn't raising middle managers who just follow orders. He is raising sons and daughters who know His business.

He has stopped giving you the Map (turn-by-turn directions) because He has handed you the **Blueprints**.

~

### Build the Fortress

Here is the hard truth about leadership: **You do not rise to the occasion; you sink to the level of your training**.

When the storm hits, when the revenue drops, when the betrayal happens, when the temptation is staring you in the face, you will not have time to go to your prayer closet for an hour to "find peace." You won't have time to wait for a sign. You will react based on what you have already built.

If you have built your life on the shifting sands of "feelings" and "signs," you will collapse. You need a structure that holds up when the lights go out. You need a **Decision Fortress**.

A Decision Fortress is a character architecture built brick by brick, long before the crisis arrives. It is constructed during the boring, invisible moments: the Tuesday afternoon at 2:30 PM when you're tired, annoyed, and want to cut a corner.

- Every time you **Arrest** a rogue thought, you lay a brick.
- Every time you **Audit** your emotions instead of venting them, you pour concrete.
- Every time you **Align** with the truth when a lie would be easier, you reinforce the walls.
- Every time you **Act** on obedience when you'd rather stay in bed, you secure the gate.

This book is your set of blueprints. We are going to walk through what I call **Watchman's Protocol**, the 4 A's (Arrest, Audit, Align, Act) that stop the spiral of panic. We are going to build the **Integrity Foundation**, the **Emotional Walls**, and the **Relational Gates**.

We are going to stop begging God to tell us *what to do*, and start becoming the kind of people He trusts to *decide*. The map is gone. The silence is here. That means the construction phase has begun.

Let's get to work.

# PART I

# THE CONSTRUCTION SITE

The silence of God is not a sign of His absence; it is the sound of a cleared job site. In the early stages of our walk, God often speaks in loud, unmistakable ways. He gives us clear signs, open doors, and direct guidance. We grow accustomed to this level of feedback. We learn to rely on the external validation of "signs" to make our decisions.

We treat God like a Magic 8-Ball, shaking Him for answers whenever we face a crossroads, but you cannot build a Fortress on a Magic 8-Ball.

There comes a time in every leader's life when the clear directions stop. The specific itinerary disappears. The voice that once boomed becomes a whisper, and then, the quiet of the construction site sets in.

This is the crisis point for many Christian leaders. We panic. We assume God has left the building. We frantically search for a new map to tell us what to do.

**You are wrong. The silence is not abandonment. It is ground-breaking.**

God withdraws the easy answers to force you to pick up the trowel. He wants you to move from being a child who needs constant hand-holding to a Master Builder who knows the Architect's mind so well that you can lay bricks without a direct command for every single movement.

In this section, we will explore why we get stuck in this silence. We will look at the danger of relying on "signs" as a crutch for character.

Most importantly, we will introduce **The Fortress Principle**: the truth that your big decisions are just the lagging indicators of the thousands of small, unseen bricks you lay every day. **You do not rise to the occasion; you sink to the level of your training.**

The Silence is where that training happens. It is where we find out if we are merely waiting for a sign, or if we are actually building the kind of structure that can withstand the storm.

**Welcome to the work site. Put on your hard hat.**

# THE DEAFENING SILENCE

I keep a physical list of monuments because I am prone to forget. I borrowed this idea from my pastor, who borrowed it from the Israelites. Whenever God parted a river or crushed an army, they did not just journal about it; they stacked stones. They built a physical structure so that when their children asked, "What do these stones mean?" they could point to the undeniable evidence of God's power.

> **Joshua 4:7** *"These stones shall be to the people of Israel a memorial forever."*

When the fog rolls in and I cannot see my hand in front of my face, I need to look back at the stones I stacked when the sun was out. One of those monuments is a check for $831.26.

We had just been hit with an unexpected expense. It was not a mortgage-ending crisis, but it was enough to knock the wind out of us. My wife and I sat at the kitchen table and did the math. I pay $833.33 per pay period in tithing, assuming no bonuses or extra income, and that was almost the exact amount of the bill. It would have been easy to skip tithing that period and use that cash to cover the expense rather than dipping into our savings. Nothing was bleeding out. We had the money, but we did not want to spend it on this bill. We debated it. The logic held; God understands math, right? We decided to pay the tithe anyway, wrote the check, and paid the bill from our savings.

Three weeks later, I opened the mailbox to find an envelope from our local public utility board. They had audited their accounts and found they had been overcharging us for years. Enclosed was a refund check for exactly $831.26. Not $830. Not $832. To the penny. I remember holding that piece of paper and feeling a terrifying sense of precision. It was not just provision; it was a flex. It was God leaning over the balcony of heaven and saying, "I am watching you. I am involved in the details. I am here."

Now, be careful here. God is not a vending machine. He does not promise a refund on every tithe, but for a spiritual child who needed to know his Father was watching, it was a kiss on the forehead.

That is the "Honeymoon Phase" of leadership. In the early days, faith feels like a technicolor movie. You pray for a parking spot, and a car pulls out. You worry about a difficult conversation, and the other person calls you first to apologize. You open your Bible randomly, and your finger lands on a verse that answers the exact question you asked three seconds ago.

I remember a day when I was drowning at work, dropping balls and feeling like a fraud. I leaned back in my chair, eyes sore and a mild headache, and Spotify auto-played

"Rest for Your Soul" by Austin French. It was the exact medicine for the exact wound at the exact moment it was needed.

It feels safe, like a parent holding a child's hand. You steer, but they balance. Every wobble is caught, and every step is guided. You could not "unsee" God if you tried.

Then, you grow up.

~

### The Fork in the Road

FAST FORWARD A FEW YEARS. The butterflies are gone, the traffic is just traffic, and the Spotify shuffle just plays random songs. You have not walked away from God; in fact, you are reading more, praying more, and serving more than ever. You are doing everything right. God goes quiet.

For me, the silence became deafening when I hit the biggest fork in the road of my career. Two offers sat on my desk.

Job A was with a well-funded startup. It was unstable, sure, but the role was contained. It was the kind of job where I could write code, clock out, and go home to be a husband and minister.

Job B was the CTO role at a twenty-year-old company. It was a disaster. The tech team was drowning, the culture was chaotic, and the ship was taking on water, but it had the title. It had the salary. It had the respect. It offered the chance to be "The Boss." I looked at Job A and saw wisdom; I looked at Job B and saw ego.

I am a Christian man, so I knew the drill for this. I did not just flip a coin; I engaged the spiritual machinery. I went to my wife, and we prayed individually and together. I waited for her to have that "check in her spirit," that super-natural intuition that wives seem to have. Instead, she came back to me and said, "I am submitting to your decision." It sounded like support, but it felt like a weight because she put it all on my shoulders.

I went to my accountability group, men who know my junk and my struggles with pride. I laid it out for them, expecting them to see the trap. They listened, asked good questions, and prayed for me. They told me to seek the Lord, so I did. I woke up early, stayed up late, and begged God for a map. *"Lord, tell me which one. If I take the startup, will it destroy my family? If I take the safe job, will I be bored? Just give me a sign. Blink the lights. Drop a check for $831.26. Anything."* I got nothing.

∾

### The Heater

I TOOK THE CTO ROLE. I started as a contractor with the plan to convert to full-time if it worked out, but it did not take long for the "heavy" to set in. The first six months were a grinder. I was working 10 to 12 hours a day, six days a week, and I was exhausted. My marriage was fraying at the edges because I was physically present but mentally absent. I tried to take a single day off to recharge, and it was interrupted by a crisis that ruined the whole day.

The company was bloated, and we had hired wrong. I had to sit in a room and fire over half the staff; good people with families. I had to look them in the eye and tell them it was over because of decisions we had made.

I remember sitting in my office one afternoon in early February. It was South Texas chilly, not Canada cold, but that damp, seeping cold that gets into your bones. The office was quiet, and I could hear the heater humming, cycling on and off. I sat there in the silence and realized: *I chose this.* I chose the title and the ego, and now I was sitting in the wreckage of that choice.

Where was God? Why did not He stop me? Why did not He block the door? A single "No" in my spirit would have saved me all of this. I felt abandoned, like I had walked out of the light and into a cave. I was wrong.

~

### The Paralysis of the Pious

WE HATE THE SILENCE. We interpret silence as "Wait" or "No," so when God does not speak, we freeze. We call it "waiting on the Lord," but often, that is just a spiritual-sounding cover for fear. We are terrified of making a mistake and terrified of being wrong.

We want a **Map**. We want turn-by-turn directions: *"Turn left at the next job offer. Merge onto the highway of ministry."* If God gives us a Map, we are not responsible for the destination. If He tells me to take the job and the company goes bankrupt, I can look at Him and say, "Well, You told me to go there. This is Your fault."

WE WANT God to be the CEO so we can be the middle manager who just executes orders. We want the safety of obedience without the risk of wisdom. God is not raising middle managers; He is raising sons and daughters.

∾

## From Instructions to Stewardship

THINK about the difference between a Junior Engineer and a Senior Engineer. It's the same difference between a medical resident and an attending physician.

When I hire a Junior Engineer, I micromanage them. I give them a specific ticket: *"Write a function that takes A and returns B. Handle these two edge cases. Do not touch the database."* I review their code constantly. If they get stuck, I jump in immediately. They don't know the system yet. They need a Map.

That is the honeymoon phase of leadership. That is God sending the $831.26 check. You are a Junior Developer, and God is kind enough to give you turn-by-turn directions.

Now consider the Senior Engineer. I don't give them a ticket. I give them a problem. *"The payment system is too slow. Please fix it."* I don't tell them how. I don't specify the tools. I don't stand over their shoulder. I leave the room. Why? I trust them.

I trust that they understand the architecture. I trust that they've internalized the principles. I trust them to make a thousand micro-decisions without my validation. That is not neglect. That is promotion.

**Silence is not abandonment. Silence is a promotion.**

God stops giving you the Map because He wants you to use the Mirror. He stops telling you *where to go* because He is focused on *who you are becoming*. He is not raising servants who require instructions for every move. He is raising sons and daughters who understand the Father's business.

When I stood at the fork between the startup and the CTO role, God didn't tell me which path to take. He was fine with either. He wasn't testing my ability to find the "right" door. He was watching how I would carry myself once I walked through one.

He didn't block the door. He let me feel the weight of leadership. Some muscles can only be built when the training wheels come off.

∼

### The Tuesday Afternoon Test

THIS IS where the rubber meets the road. It is easy to be a "Christian leader" on Sunday morning when the worship band is playing, but it is hard to be a Christian leader on a Tuesday afternoon when the server crashes, the customer is screaming, and you are hemorrhaging money. In that moment, you do not have time to go to the prayer closet for an hour. You do not get a writing on the wall. You get silence.

What do you do? Do you freeze? Do you panic? Or do you reach into the reservoir of character you have built over the years and make a decision?

The goal of this book is not to help you find the Map. The Map does not exist. The goal is to help you build the internal operating system (the Mirror) that allows you to stand in the silence and lead with wisdom. To move from the paralysis of "What is God's Will?" to the governance of "I am doing God's Will by who I am being."

It is time to stop waiting for a sign. It is time to start building the stronghold.

## 2

## THE MAGIC 8-BALL GOD

D o you remember the Magic 8-Ball? It was that black plastic sphere filled with blue dye. You would ask it a question, shake it violently, and wait for the little blue triangle to float to the surface. "Signs point to yes." "Reply hazy, try again." If you did not like the answer you simply shook again it until you did. It was a toy, but for many of us, it became our theology.

We treat God like a cosmic vending machine of decision-making data. We input a request: "Should we acquire this competitor?" We shake the spiritual 8-Ball by fasting, playing worship music, or waiting for a "feeling." Then we stare at the surface of our lives, waiting for the blue triangle to appear. We call this "seeking God's will," but often, it is actually an attempt to bypass the hard work of wisdom. We want an answer; God wants to build an instinct.

~

## The "Peace" Trap

THE MOST COMMON "BLUE TRIANGLE" we look for is peace. We say things like, "I prayed about it, and I felt peace." The problem is that peace is a terrible barometer for truth when used in isolation. Jonah felt enough peace to fall asleep in the boat while running directly against God's command. His peace was delusion.

> **Jonah 1:5** *"But Jonah had gone down into the inner part of the ship and had lain down and was fast asleep."*

Conversely, Jesus sweat blood in Gethsemane. He was in perfect alignment with God's will, yet He felt zero emotional comfort. He felt agony.

> **Luke 22:44** *"And being in agony he prayed more earnestly; and his sweat became like great drops of blood falling down to the ground."*

I learned this the hard way in 2023, shortly after I became a believer. I had joined a small men's group that met every Tuesday morning at 6:30 AM. **Best time of the day!**

Sometimes we read a book together; other times we studied a book of the Bible. After about six months, the leader, and pastor, asked if we would be interested in putting on a men's event at our church because the need was desperate. Little did I know, this single event would turn into a full blown men's ministry.

The group agreed, but no one stepped up to lead it. Given my background in business and my "youthful vigor" (spiritually speaking), I decided to take the reins. I was a young believer, and the Bible warns about this in 1 Timothy 3:6, stating that a leader should not be a recent convert lest he become puffed up with conceit. I was most definitely a leader in this situation, and I struggled to comprehend what was happening.

> 1 **Timothy 3:6** *"An elder must not be a new believer, because he might become proud, and the devil would cause him to fall."*

Why would God put me in a leadership role when I had only been a believer for less than a year? Was I moving too fast? Was this God putting this on my heart, or was this my worldly ambition at play? Worse, was it the devil trying to mislead me and cause me to fail in my spiritual journey? I really struggled to understand if this was God, me, or the enemy speaking.

After we planned most of the event, I was asked to speak and tell my story. I initially said no because it felt like too much, but I later agreed. It went amazingly well considering it was my first public message about Jesus. Looking back all glory to God. I had nothing to do with this. I had plenty of speaking experience, but never about God, but He built a monument that day!

However, the internal battle was chaos. My wife warned me repeatedly because I would say things like, "come to **MY** event." I was taking ownership, but in a prideful way. It was a slippery slope.

I believe God was urging me to do it, but He also knew I needed a strong support group around me to prevent my ego from taking hold. If I had relied solely on "feeling peace," I would have been lost because I felt everything but peace. I felt conflict, pride, and fear all at once.

∾

## Map vs. Mirror

WE ASK GOD FOR A MAP. We want to know where to go, which job to take, and who to marry. We want the 5-year strategy laid out on a table.

God hands us a **Mirror**. He asks, "Who are you becoming?" He asks if you are honest, if you govern your temper, and if you are faithful with the little things.

God is often silent on the **Geography** (The Map) because He is focused on the **Geometry** (The Mirror).

He knows that if He sends you to the "Promised Land" (the calling He has for you, whether that is a palace or a prison), before you have the character to sustain it, the blessing will crush you.

Consider the Israelites. They left Egypt and wanted a straight line to Canaan. God kept them in the wilderness for forty years. It was not just punishment; it was preparation.

> **Deuteronomy 8:2** *"And you shall remember the whole way that the Lord your God has led you these forty years in the wilderness, that he might humble you, testing you to know what was in your heart."*

They had left Egypt, but Egypt had not left them. They still had "slave minds" filled with fear, scarcity, and complaining. If God had dropped them into Canaan immediately, they would have destroyed it, or been destroyed. The wilderness was the Mirror. It revealed who they were so God could deal with it.

You might be frustrated because the promotion is

delayed. You are shaking the 8-Ball asking "When?" God is holding up the Mirror asking "Are you ready?"

~

### Sons vs. Servants

WHY DOES God dislike the 8-Ball approach? It requires zero relationship. You do not have to know the toy; you just have to shake it.

God is not looking for servants who need explicit instructions for every task. "Do this. Then do that." He is raising sons and daughters who know the Father's heart. A son can make decisions that honor the father without needing a memo for every move.

God hides the Map to force us to learn His heart. He wants us to lead like heirs, not like employees waiting for instructions.

~

### The Tuesday Afternoon Test

THIS BRINGS us to the Tuesday Afternoon Test. How do you apply this when money is on the line?

I was working at a startup, and we hired a marketing agency to put together a comprehensive marketing strategy. They were the "best" in the industry and charged a premium for it.

We were a smaller account for them, and ultimately, we did not get their A-team, but we certainly paid for it.

Six weeks went by, and nothing had been delivered. We

had plenty of wasted time, wasted calls, and broken promises. We had missed our window of opportunity.

I did not pray for them to quit. I prayed that the situation would "resolve itself." I prayed that they would suddenly deliver on their work and promises so we could come to an agreement.

I do not like conflict, so I avoid it. I was shaking the 8-Ball, hoping for a magical "Yes" that would save me from having a hard conversation. It did not happen. The silence continued.

I finally had to have the conversation. I told them that too much time had passed and that we were going to cancel our contract. It was tense. I had to be forceful.

Ultimately, they refunded most of our money. We agreed to pay a small portion for the time spent. I walked away from that call knowing I had handled it correctly. I did not need a burning bush to tell me to be a good steward of the company's money. I needed the character to stand in the conflict and resolve it with integrity.

So, if we cannot rely on the Magic 8-Ball, how do we make decisions? We have to build a new mechanism.


WE HAVE to start laying bricks in our fortress.

# 3

# THE FORTRESS PRINCIPLE

We love movies where the underdog rises to the occasion in the final act. We believe that when the big test comes, the firing, the lawsuit, the moral dilemma, we will summon a reserve of strength we have not built. We think we can be lazy in training and heroic in the battle.

The reality is that **you do not rise to the occasion; you sink to the level of your training**.

In a crisis, you do not think; you react. Your reaction is determined by your "Default Settings," which are programmed by the thousands of small choices you made when no one was watching.

You cannot "decide" to have a fortress in the middle of an invasion any more than you can "decide" to run a marathon the morning of the race. You have to have built the capacity beforehand.

~

## The Fortress Principle

ALIGNMENT IS NOT A LIGHTNING BOLT; it is compound interest. This is the **Fortress Principle:** You do not build the walls in the middle of the war. You build them brick by brick, decision by decision, on a boring Tuesday.

Every time you make a decision, you are placing a brick on the wall. You do not bake the bricks; God's grace provides them, but you must lift them.

- One brick offers no protection.
- Ten bricks create a tripping hazard.
- **Ten thousand bricks build a Fortress that can withstand a storm.**

Most people think of "decisions" as the big forks in the road: who to marry, which job to take, or whether to move to a new city. Those are not decisions; those are *outcomes*. The real decisions are the microscopic choices you make a hundred times a day.

- When you choose to wake up at 6:00 AM instead of hitting snooze, you lay a **Brick of Discipline.**
- When you choose to tell your wife the truth about a small frustration instead of burying it, you lay a **Brick of Intimacy.**
- When you choose to admit you do not know the answer in a meeting instead of faking it, you lay a **Brick of Humility.**

The invisible work is what matters. Ninety-nine percent

of Fortress Building happens when no one is watching. It is the choice to not send the snarky email. It is the choice to turn off the screen. It is the choice to tell the truth about a five-dollar mistake so you can tell the truth about a $350,000 mistake.

~

## Cracked Bricks and Weak Mortar

THIS WORKS IN REVERSE, too. You can build a fortress, or you can build a prison. Every time you cut a corner, you lay a **Brick of Compromise**. Every time you shade the truth to look better, you lay a **Brick of Deceit**.

Eventually, you build a wall so high that you cannot see over it, and you wonder why you feel trapped.

The goal is to build a Fortress so high and so thick that when the crisis comes, your "Default Setting" is automatic. You do not have to *try* to be honest; you simply *are* honest because that is the wall you have built.

~

## Character Is a Lagging Indicator

IN FINANCE, "REVENUE" is a lagging indicator. It tells you what happened in sales and marketing ninety days ago. You cannot fix Q3 revenue in the last week of Q3. If the number is bad, it is because the work three months ago was bad.

**Character is the lagging indicator of your Fortress Building.**

If you snap at your wife today, it is not just because you had a bad day; it is because your "Patience Wall" is weak. If you withstand a massive ethical pressure at work, it is because your "Integrity Foundation" is deep.

I learned this the hard way with a $350,000 mistake. A client was mis-billed nearly 1,000 hours. When the pressure came to hide it, I caved. I failed not because the pressure was unique, but because my Integrity Foundation was too shallow. I had not built enough "small truth" bricks to withstand the "big lie" pressure.

I tried to be a Crisis Hero, and I found out that I was just a man living in a straw hut.

~

### Stewardship of the Small

SCRIPTURE IS clear on this principle.

> *Luke 16:10 "One who is faithful in a very little is also faithful in much, and one who is dishonest in a very little is also dishonest in much."*

Note that it does not say "One who is faithful in little *will become* faithful in much." It implies they are the same thing. The "Much" is just the "Little" under a magnifying glass.

David did not kill Goliath because he suddenly got brave. He killed Goliath because he had been killing lions and bears in the wilderness when only sheep were watching.

He built his Fortress in private so he could stand in it in public.

~

## The Tuesday Afternoon Test

WE WAIT FOR THE "BIG DECISION" (the job, the move, the marriage) to start aligning with God. We think we will get serious when the stakes are high.

The reality is that you are building your Fortress right now. Reading this page is laying a brick.

It is easy to be faithful on Sunday morning when you are surrounded by your Christian brothers and sisters. It is easy to be faithful in the crisis when the adrenaline is pumping and everyone is watching.

It is much harder to be faithful on a Tuesday afternoon at 2:30 PM when you are tired, bored, and annoyed.

This is the construction site. This is where the real work happens. God is not waiting for your big performance on the stage; He is watching your small obedience in the cubicle.

**If you cannot be faithful in the quiet, boring moments of a Tuesday, you will not be faithful in the loud, chaotic moments of a crisis.**

Identify one "Brick" you need to lay today.

- Is it an apology you need to make?
- Is it replacing a bad habit with a good one?
- Is it arresting a thought before it becomes an action?

Stop trying to fix the fruit. Start fixing the root. **Start building the Fortress.**

**4**

# WHAT IF I CHOOSE WRONG?

This is the question no one asks out loud. We dress it up in spiritual language. We call it *discernment*. We call it *wisdom*. We call it *waiting on the Lord*, but underneath all of it is a quieter, more honest fear:

- What if I act in good faith... and still mess it up?
- What if I choose the wrong job?
- What if I marry the wrong person?
- What if I take the risk and it collapses?
- What if I step forward and God doesn't catch me?

For many Christian leaders, this fear becomes paralyzing. We are not rebellious. We are not lazy. We are afraid of being wrong in front of God. So we freeze.

We wait for a feeling. We wait for peace. We wait for a sign. We stand at the fork in the road, staring down both paths, terrified that one wrong step will permanently derail God's plan for our lives. This fear feels holy, but it is not.

∾

## The Myth of the One Right Door

MANY OF US secretly believe that God's will is a single, fragile path. One correct door among a thousand wrong doors. Miss it, and you are forever outside the plan.

This belief turns decision-making into a minefield. If I step wrong, I fail God. If I fail God, I lose His favor. If I lose His favor, everything collapses.

So we outsource responsibility back to Him. We beg for certainty because certainty absolves us of ownership.

"If God tells me what to do, and it goes badly, at least it wasn't my fault." Scripture does not present God's will as a tightrope. It presents it as a **relationship**. God is far more interested in *how* you walk than *which sidewalk* you choose.

∾

## Wrong Is Not the Same as Sinful

HERE IS a critical distinction most leaders never make: **A decision can be wrong without being sinful.**

Choosing Job A instead of Job B is not sin. Launching the product and missing the market is not sin. Taking the role and discovering you were unprepared is not sin.

Sin is disobedience. Sin is compromise. Sin is violating truth, integrity, or love to protect yourself. God does not punish His children for imperfect judgment. He disciplines them for rebellion and pride.

When we confuse *mistakes* with *sin*, we turn God into a fragile taskmaster instead of a faithful Father. A father does not disown his child for falling while learning to walk. He watches how they get back up.

~

## The Real Question God Is Asking

WHEN YOU STAND at a fork in the road, God is rarely asking: "Did you pick the perfect option?"

HE IS ASKING:

- "Will you govern yourself when it gets hard?"
- "Will you tell the truth when it costs you?"
- "Will you stay humble when you succeed?"
- "Will you stay faithful when you fail?"

God did not block doors for David. He did not micromanage Joseph's career path. He did not tell Paul where every road would lead.

He watched their character under pressure. A bad decision can be redeemed. A compromised character must be rebuilt.

~

## Failure Is Not Proof You Missed God

SOME OF THE most formative moments in Scripture came *after* a "wrong" decision.

David chose to stay home when kings go to war. That decision led to catastrophe. God did not abandon him. He confronted him, restored him, and used the failure to deepen his leadership.

2 Samuel 11:1-5 *"In the spring of the year, when kings normally go out to war, David sent Joab and the Israelite army to fight the Ammonites. They destroyed the Ammonite army and laid siege to the city of Rabbah. However, David stayed behind in Jerusalem. Late one afternoon, after his midday rest, David got out of bed and was walking on the roof of the palace. As he looked out over the city, he noticed a woman of unusual beauty taking a bath. He sent someone to find out who she was, and he was told, "She is Bathsheba, the daughter of Eliam and the wife of Uriah the Hittite." Then David sent messengers to get her; and when she came to the palace, he slept with her. She had just completed the purification rites after having her menstrual period. Then she returned home. Later, when Bathsheba discovered that she was pregnant, she sent David a message, saying, "I'm pregnant.""*

Peter chose courage in the wrong moment and denied Christ. Jesus did not revoke his calling. He repaired the breach and gave him greater responsibility.

Luke 22:54-62 *"So they arrested him and led him to the high priest's home. And Peter followed at a distance. The guards lit a fire in the middle of the courtyard and sat around it, and Peter joined them there. A servant girl noticed him in the firelight and began staring at him. Finally she said, "This man was one of Jesus' followers!" But Peter denied it. "Woman," he said, "I don't even know him!" After a while someone else looked at him and said, "You must be one of them!" "No, man, I'm not!" Peter retorted. About an hour later someone else insisted, "This must be one of them, because he is a Galilean, too." But Peter said,*

*"Man, I don't know what you are talking about." And immediately, while he was still speaking, the rooster crowed. At that moment the Lord turned and looked at Peter. Suddenly, the Lord's words flashed through Peter's mind: "Before the rooster crows tomorrow morning, you will deny three times that you even know me." And Peter left the courtyard, weeping bitterly."*

God is not surprised by your learning curve. He is not waiting to disqualify you. He is watching to see if you will repent, repair, and keep building.

～

### Paralysis Is the Real Danger

HERE IS THE UNCOMFORTABLE TRUTH: **Indecision is usually more destructive than imperfect action.**

Paralysis trains fear. Delay erodes confidence. Avoidance builds a habit of surrendering leadership. When you refuse to decide, you are still choosing. You are choosing comfort over courage, safety over stewardship.

The servant who buried the talent was not condemned for losing it. He was condemned for doing nothing with it. God can steer a moving leader. He cannot steer a statue.

∾

## Faithfulness Over Accuracy

THE GOAL of leadership is not to be flawless. The goal is to be faithful.

FAITHFULNESS LOOKS LIKE THIS:

- Making the best decision you can with the information you have.
- Running it through truth, counsel, and conscience.
- Owning the outcome without blaming God or others.
- Repairing quickly when you fail.

That is not recklessness. That is maturity. God does not demand perfection. He demands **alignment**.

∾

## Why the Protocol Comes Next

THIS IS why you need a protocol. Not to guarantee perfect outcomes. Not to eliminate risk. Not to protect you from ever being wrong.

You need a protocol to ensure that **who you become** is never wrong, even when the decision is imperfect. The Watchman's Protocol does not promise success. It promises integrity under pressure. That is something God can build on.

# 5

# WHEN THERE IS NO PROTOCOL

Competence is a dangerous thing without structure. Most leadership failures do not begin with bad intentions. They begin with capable people reacting in real time, under pressure, without a system to govern themselves.

They are smart. They are experienced. They care deeply about the outcome, and when the crisis hits, they improvise.

~

### The Illusion of "I'll Figure It Out"

HIGH PERFORMERS ARE ESPECIALLY vulnerable to this trap. They have succeeded before without a framework. They trust their instincts. They believe pressure sharpens them. They tell themselves, *"I'll rise to the occasion."* Pressure does not create character. Pressure **reveals** it.

When you rely on instinct alone, your default setting takes over. Fear gets louder. Ego gets faster. Old habits reclaim authority. In a crisis, you do not become more thoughtful. You become more *you*.

~

## A Leader Without a Protocol

PICTURE A CAPABLE LEADER facing a sudden crisis. The client threatens to walk. The board is demanding answers. The team is panicking. There is no pause. No framework. No gate.

The email gets sent too quickly. The tone sharpens. The facts are bent "just a little." Blame is redirected. Control replaces clarity.

None of it feels evil in the moment. It feels *necessary*. This is how trust erodes. This is how cultures turn brittle. This is how leaders lose themselves one reaction at a time. Not because they are bad leaders. but because they are **unguarded leaders**.

~

## Reaction Is Not Leadership

REACTION FEELS PRODUCTIVE. It feels decisive. It feels strong. Reaction is not leadership. Reaction is surrender. It is letting the loudest emotion at the moment take the wheel.

Anger masquerades as conviction. Urgency disguises fear. Silence hides cowardice. Without a protocol, every situation becomes a referendum on your emotional state, and emotions are terrible commanders.

~

## The Cost You Don't See Until Later

THE MOST DANGEROUS part of ungoverned leadership is that it often *works*, at first. The crisis is averted. The deal is saved. The meeting ends, but the cost is deferred.

Authority leaks. Trust thins. The team learns what moods to avoid. You begin managing perceptions instead of reality. Months later, you wonder why everything feels fragile. The fortress was never built. You've just been standing in the open, hoping the storm misses you.

~

## Why Good Intentions Aren't Enough

MANY LEADERS BELIEVE sincerity is protection.

- *"My heart is in the right place."*
- *"I didn't mean it that way."*
- *"I was under a lot of pressure."*

Intentions matter, but they do not govern behavior.

A pilot does not rely on sincerity in a storm. A surgeon does not improvise under pressure. A soldier does not "go with their gut" in combat. They rely on protocols. Not because they are weak, but because they understand human limits.

~

## You Already Have a Protocol. It's Just Invisible

HERE IS THE UNCOMFORTABLE TRUTH: If you don't choose a protocol, **you still have one**. It's just undocumented.

Your real protocol might be:

- Avoid conflict
- Assert control
- Protect image
- Delay truth
- React fast, apologize later

That system is running every time pressure hits. The question is not *whether* you have a protocol. The question is whether it is **worthy of governing your life**.

~

## Why Structure is a Form of Mercy

A PROTOCOL DOES NOT REMOVE responsibility. It removes chaos. It gives you a place to stand when emotions surge. It slows the moment just enough for wisdom to speak. It protects you from becoming the threat you fear.

A protocol is not legalism. It is mercy. For you and for the people you lead.

~

## The Threshold

IF YOU ARE willing to admit that instinct is not enough, if you are willing to stop improvising your integrity, if you are ready to govern yourself before you try to govern others, then you are ready for a protocol.

Not one built on feelings. Not one built on fear. One built to stand in silence, pressure, and uncertainty. That protocol comes next.

# PART II

# THE WATCHMAN'S PROTOCOL (THE 4 A'S)

If the map is gone, how do we move? If the voice is silent, how do we decide? We need a protocol.

In high-stakes environments like aviation, medicine, special operations, professionals don't rely on "feeling" their way through a crisis. They rely on protocols. They have checklists and training that guides their actions when the pressure is high and the information is incomplete.

The Christian life is no different. When we are in the Silence, we cannot rely on our fluctuating emotions or our limited understanding. We need a reliable framework for self-governance. We need a way to bypass our default reactions, which are usually fear-based or self-protective, and access the mind of Christ.

This section introduces **The Watchman's Protocol**, a four-step heuristic designed to help you navigate the fog of decision-making:

1. **ARREST:** Stopping the momentum of your spiraling thoughts. You must become the Sheriff of your own mind, taking every thought captive before it takes you captive.
2. **AUDIT:** brutally examine the source of your anxiety. Are you turning Inward to your own limited resources, or Upward to the Source of all wisdom? It requires the vulnerability to admit, "I usually turn inward."
3. **ALIGN:** Re-calibrating your heart to the Truth. This is about using a Compass, not a Map. It is about finding direction in places like Scripture, counsel, and the quiet promptings of the Spirit, rather than demanding a turn-by-turn itinerary.
4. **ACT:** Moving forward with obedience in the dark. Faith is not knowing the outcome; it is taking the next step because you trust the One who leads you.

The Watchman's Protocol is not a magic spell. It is a discipline. It is the practical "how-to" of walking by faith and not by sight. It is how we learn to lead ourselves so that we can effectively lead others.

# 6

# THE WATCHMAN'S PROTOCOL

A fortress without a gatekeeper is just a ruin waiting to happen. You can have the thickest walls and the deepest foundations. You can have the **Integrity Foundation** poured with reinforced concrete. You can have **Emotional Walls** high enough to keep out a flood, but if the gates are left wide open, the enemy simply walks in.

In ancient times, the safety of the city depended entirely on the **Watchman**. He stood at the highest point of the wall. He was responsible for identifying threats while they were still far off, distinguishing between a returning friend and an approaching foe.

Most importantly, he controlled the mechanism of the gate.

∿

### The Blood on Your Hands

IN THE BOOK OF EZEKIEL, God defines the weight of this role:

> "If the watchman sees the sword coming and does not blow the
> trumpet to warn the people and the sword comes and takes
> someone's life, that person's life will be taken because of their sin,
> but I will hold the watchman accountable for their blood."
> (Ezekiel 33:6)

Being a Watchman is not a passive role. It is a matter of
life and death.

∿

### You are the Watchman of your own mind.

YOU CANNOT STOP the threats from approaching. You live in
a fallen world. You cannot stop the sudden surge of anger
when a client insults you. You cannot stop the flash of lust,
the whisper of panic, or the wave of insecurity from walking
up to the gate of your mind, but you have the authority to
stop them from entering.

The mistake most people make is believing they are
helpless against their own thoughts. "I just got angry," they
say, as if the anger was a weather event that happened to
them.

No! The anger approached the gate, and the Watchman
was asleep, so it walked right into the throne room and sat
down.

You need a Standing Order. You need a protocol for the gate.

~

## The Watchman's Protocol

I CALL this **The Watchman's Protocol**. It is not a suggestion; it is your operating procedure for gate duty. It is how you translate the abstract idea of "self-control" into a mechanical process of defense.

It consists of four distinct movements: **Arrest**, **Audit**, **Align**, and **Act**.

### 1. ARREST (Halt at the Gate)

The first job of the Watchman is to stop momentum. Sin and panic have kinetic energy. They move fast. If you don't stop them at the perimeter, they gain speed. By the time the thought becomes an action, it is often too late to stop it.

**ARREST** is the moment the Watchman sees a stranger approaching and crosses his spear. He shouts, *"Halt! Who goes there?"* He physically bars the entry mechanism.

In leadership, this looks like the "Pause." It is the split second between the stimulus (the rude email) and the response (the snarky reply). It is the moment you feel the heat rise in your chest or the knot form in your stomach.

You cannot audit a thought that is moving at 100 mph. You have to arrest it first.

Close the laptop. Take a breath. Walk out of the room. Do whatever you have to do to stop the train.

.  .  .

## 2. AUDIT (Check Credentials)

Once the stranger is halted at the gate, the Watchman does not just let them in because they look urgent. He interrogates them.

**AUDIT** is the interrogation phase. The Watchman asks: *"Are you a friend or a foe? Did the King send you, or did the Enemy send you?"*

Most of our thoughts are liars. They arrive dressed as "Urgency" or "Righteous Indignation," but underneath, they are Fear and Pride.

- **The Thought:** *"We are going to go bankrupt if we don't sign this deal."*
- **The Audit:** Is that a fact (friend/intel) or a fear (foe/lie)? Do I have data to support that, or am I just panicking?.

- **The Thought:** *"I need to put this employee in their place."*
- **The Audit:** Is that leadership (correction) or is that ego (revenge)?

The Watchman demands to see the papers. If the credentials don't check out, the gate stays shut.

## 3. ALIGN (Check Standing Orders)

The Watchman does not make the rules. He enforces them. When a visitor arrives, the Watchman doesn't ask, "Do I feel like letting this person in?" No! He consults the King's Decree. (Scripture, counsel, etc.)

**ALIGN** is checking the Compass. It is holding the impulse up against the standard of Truth.

If the impulse is to lie to a client to cover a mistake, the Watchman checks the Standing Orders.

- *The Order:* "Lying lips are an abomination to the Lord" (Proverbs 12:22).
- *The Decision:* Entry denied.

It doesn't matter if the lie would save you money. It doesn't matter if it would be convenient. The Standing Order is clear. The Watchman aligns with the King, not the circumstances.

### 4. ACT (Operate the Gate)

This is the kinetic step. The Watchman cannot just stand there analyzing; he must operate the mechanism.

**ACT** is the decisive movement.

- **If it is a Friend (Truth):** Crank the gate open. Let it in. Embrace the hard truth. Walk into the boss's office and admit the mistake.
- **If it is a Foe (Lie):** Sound the alarm. Drive it away. Delete the email draft. Rebuke the fear.

This step requires sweat. Knowing the truth isn't enough; you have to let the truth in. Knowing the lie isn't enough; you have to kick the lie out.

∾

## The Sleeping Watchman

WHAT HAPPENS when you skip the Protocol?

When you don't **Arrest**, you react emotionally. When you don't **Audit**, you believe lies. When you don't **Align**, you build on sand. When you don't **Act**, you remain paralyzed.

A fortress with a sleeping Watchman is just a warehouse for the enemy's supplies. If you are tired of being overrun by anxiety, fear, and reactionary leadership, it is time to wake up. Climb the tower. Take your post.

The Protocol is simple, but it is not easy. It requires vigilance. It requires the discipline to do it on a Tuesday afternoon when no one is watching and nothing seems to be happening. That is when the enemy scouts the walls.


IT IS **time to stand watch.**

# 7

# ARREST (STOPPING THE MOMENTUM)

S in has momentum. Sin is like a heavy train rolling downhill. It does not stop on its own; it must be actively arrested.

I am ashamed to say that my flesh has gotten the best of me many times. I fail at this weekly. I choose to look at a member of the opposite sex with lust. I tell small white lies to avoid inconvenience. I allow my words to cut when I feel disrespected. I choose football over church.

I used to have an addiction to pornography. It was just a normal part of my day. The first thing I would do in the morning was look at porn. It was automatic. My brain was on a track: Wake up -> Grab phone -> Connect to VPN -> Browse Reddit -> Sin.

I did not realize how much those small habits were ruining my life, my marriage, and my relationship with God. I was letting the train roll.

After I became a believer, I realized I could not just "try harder" to stop the train. I had to derail it. I uninstalled the VPN from my PC. I uninstalled the Reddit app. I put the Bible app where the Reddit app used to live on my Home

Screen. I replaced the morning ritual. Instead of turning to Reddit first thing, I turned to the Bible App. I uninstalled all social media apps. As I changed my fleshly momentum, my entire view of women and life began to change.

~

## You Are the Sheriff

WE OFTEN USE THE WORD "PAUSE" when talking about self-control. "Just pause and count to ten." The problem is that "Pause" sounds passive. It sounds like waiting.

We need a stronger word. We need **ARREST**.

"Arrest" is active. It implies authority. It implies a crime is in progress, a crime against wisdom, love, or patience. You are the Sheriff of your mind, deputized by the King.

> **2 Corinthians 10:5** *"We destroy arguments and every lofty opinion raised against the knowledge of God, and take every thought captive to obey Christ."*

"Captive" is military language. It means taking a prisoner of war. You do not negotiate with a rogue thought; you tackle it and put it in handcuffs.

You are not your thoughts. You are the *thinker* of your thoughts. You have the authority to stand outside the impulse and say, "You are not the conductor of this train!"

~

## The Trigger

YOUR BODY usually knows you are about to sin before your brain does. You need to learn to recognize the physical cues of the momentum building.

- The tightness in the chest.
- The heat in the face.
- The rapid typing speed.
- The shallow breathing.

There are emotional cues, too. The most dangerous one is the sudden urgency to be "understood" immediately. You feel a desperate need to "set the record straight" right now.

**Urgency is rarely the Holy Spirit.** Wisdom rarely screams; panic and pride do.

~

## Physical Disruption

YOU CANNOT THINK your way out of a physiological hijack. You have to move. You have to physically disrupt the momentum.

1. **Hands Off:** Physically remove your hands from the keyboard or the phone. You cannot sin digitally if you are not touching the device.
2. **The Laptop:** Close the laptop lid. Do not just minimize the window; shut the machine. The

    sound of the lid snapping shut is a gavel hitting the desk.

3. **The Verbal Command:** Say "STOP" out loud. It sounds crazy, but it engages a different part of your brain. It breaks the internal loop of rationalization.

4. **The Phone Drop:** Do not just set it down gently. Toss it onto the other cushion of the couch. Create immediate distance.

5. **The Physiological Reset:** Splash cold water on your face or do ten pushups. Your body is flooded with "fight or flight" adrenaline; give it something to do other than sin.

6. **The Environment Switch:** Step outside. Sunlight and fresh air are natural disinfectants for a dark mood. Leave the room where the temptation lives.

**James 1:19** *"Know this, my beloved brothers: let every person be quick to hear, slow to speak, slow to anger."*

"Slow" is not a personality speed; it is a governance brake. Some people are naturally slow processors. That is not what James is talking about. He is talking about the intentional mechanical action of applying the brakes to a spinning wheel.

It creates the gap between *Stimulus* and *Response*. In that gap, you have freedom. Without the gap, you are just a machine reacting to inputs.

Someone insults you (Input) -> You insult them back (Output). That is not leadership; that is an algorithm. The "Slow" is the moment you step in and say, "I am not a machine. I am a son of God, and I choose how I respond."

~

### "But I Have to Be Authentic"

CULTURE TELLS US THAT "AUTHENTICITY" means expressing every feeling we have in real-time. We are told that if we feel angry, we must show it, and if we feel hurt, we must say it. We have conflated "honesty" with a "lack of filter." We believe that holding back a thought is a form of deception, and that the most "real" version of ourselves is the one that reacts instantly to every impulse.

**That is a lie.** Unfiltered authenticity is just immaturity. Toddlers are the most authentic people on the planet; they scream when they are hungry, hit when they are mad, and cry when they are tired. They hold nothing back. Yet, we do not let toddlers run companies, and we do not let them lead families. Leaders are *governed*. A leader is someone who feels the scream rising in their throat and chooses to swallow it for the good of the room.

We do not want to be "authentic" to our flesh; we want to be "authentic" to our convictions. If my core value is kindness, but my current emotion is rage, then acting on the rage is actually *inauthentic* to who I really am or want to be. It is a betrayal of my values in favor of my chemistry. Arresting a thought is not being fake; it is being faithful to the person you have decided to be.

～

## The Tuesday Afternoon Test

I HAD a recent interaction with a particularly difficult co-worker from a partner company. He is brash, extremely rough around the edges, and cutting with nearly every remark. He is the type of person you dread getting on a call with.

One day, he was being extremely brash on a call with many people. He targeted a female co-worker whom I have a lot of respect for. Everyone does. Normally, I remain quiet on these calls and allow the team to handle things, but this day I wanted to explode. I wanted to cut back. I wanted to protect my team with rage. I felt the heat. I felt the momentum. I arrested it.

Instead of exploding, I kept my composure. I interrupted him in a polite but firm way. I said, "Please treat my staff with respect and refrain from these remarks. If you cannot do that, we will reschedule the call to a later time with a different rep."

He apologized. The call continued in a much more respectful manner. I did not win by out-shouting him; I won by arresting my own flesh so I could lead with authority.

Okay, you have stopped the train. You have arrested the rogue thought. It is sitting in the back of the squad car in handcuffs. Now what? You have to interrogate it.

# 8

# AUDIT (INTERROGATING THE IMPULSE)

The cave was dark, damp, and smelled of fear. Six hundred men held their breath, pressed against the cold limestone walls of En Gedi.

Then, the silhouette appeared. King Saul. The man who had hunted them like dogs. The man who had stripped David of his wife, his home, and his rigorous service record. Saul entered the cave alone to relieve himself, completely vulnerable.

In the darkness, David's men whispered the words that every leader wants to hear:

1 Samuel 24:4 *"Here is the day of which the Lord said to you, 'Behold, I will give your enemy into your hand, and you shall do to him as it shall seem good to you.'"*

It was the perfect setup. It was logical. It was efficient. It even sounded spiritual. The circumstances aligned perfectly with the "Map." If David killed Saul right now, the civil war would end. David would be king. Israel would have peace.

David crept forward, knife in hand. He reached out... and cut off the corner of Saul's robe.

Then, something happened that separates the Kings from the conquerors:

> 1 Samuel 24:5 *"And afterward David's heart struck him, because he had cut off a corner of Saul's robe."*

David stopped. He backed away. He audited the impulse. His men were furious, they wanted blood, but David saw something they didn't. He saw that killing Saul would be an **Inward** victory, not an **Upward** one. He would have the crown, but he would have lost his integrity.

This is the power of the Audit. It is the split-second interrogation of an impulse that looks right, feels right, and even sounds "Christian," but is actually a trap.

∾

### The False Map

DAVID'S MEN made the classic mistake of the High Performer: they interpreted *opportunity* as *permission*.

They looked at the data:

1. Target acquired.
2. Defenses down.
3. Prophecy (allegedly) fulfilled.
4. Execute.

Most of us run our careers this way. We see an open door, and we assume God opened it. We see a competitor stumble, and we assume it is our time to take market share.

We see a subordinate make a mistake, and we assume it is our job to crush them with "accountability," but an open door is not always a mandate. Sometimes, it is a test.

~

### Inward vs. Upward

WHEN THE PRESSURE HITS, when the email lands, when the server crashes, when the client threatens to walk, you have a choice. You can turn Inward, or you can turn Upward.

**The Inward Audit (The Default)**

The Inward Audit is the default operating system for competent leaders. It relies on your resources, your logic, and your grit.

- "Can I handle this?"
- "What is the most efficient solution?"
- "How do I win?"

If David had used the Inward Audit, he would have killed Saul. It was the "smart" play. It was low risk, high reward, but the Inward Audit has a fatal flaw: it is limited by *your* perspective. It prioritizes short-term relief (killing the enemy) over long-term character (honoring God's anointed).

**The Upward Audit (The Crown)**

The Upward Audit ignores the odds and examines the Source.

- "Does this align with God's character?"
- "Am I bypassing the process?"
- "If I win this way, do I lose myself?"

David realized that grabbing the kingdom by force was a shortcut. It was an attempt to do God's work without God's timing.

∼

### Ego vs. Righteousness

THE HARDEST PART of the Audit is that our flesh loves to dress up as the Spirit. We rarely say, "I am going to yield to my massive ego right now." No, we say, "I am going to stand up for the truth." We disguise **Ego** as **Righteousness**.

Let's look at a modern example: **The Righteous Crusade.** You have a team member who drops the ball. They miss a deadline that makes you look bad to the Board. You feel the heat rising in your chest. You type out a "clarifying email." You copy their boss. You use words like "unacceptable," "standard of excellence," and "stewardship."

You tell yourself you are protecting the culture. You tell yourself you are holding the line.

### The Audit:

- *The Action:* Sending the public rebuke.
- *The Label:* "High Standards."
- *The Reality:* You are embarrassed. You are scared. You are punishing them to make yourself feel powerful again.

I have sent that email, and just like David with the robe, my heart struck me afterward. I wasn't leading; I was venting. I wasn't fixing the problem; I was managing my image.

If it is Ego, the goal is *Vindication*. If it is Righteousness, the goal is *Restoration*.

∼

### The Diagnostic: Two Levels

HOW DO you catch this in real-time? How do you replicate David's restraint in the cave when you are in the boardroom? You need a diagnostic checklist.

### Level 1: The Biological Audit (H.A.L.T.)

Before you spiritualize the problem, assume you are just a biology experiment gone wrong. The recovery community (AA) gave us the H.A.L.T. method, and it saves careers.

- Hungry: Low blood sugar looks a lot like "righteous indignation."
- Angry: Are you carrying frustration from the previous meeting?
- Lonely: Do you feel isolated and defensive?
- Tired: Fatigue makes cowards of us all.

If you are H.A.L.T., do not send the email. Do not make the decision. Eat a sandwich. Take a nap. Elijah the Prophet needed a snack and a nap before he could hear God (1 Kings 19). You are not stronger than Elijah.

**Level 2: The Motive Audit**

ONCE YOU ARE FED and rested, if the impulse is still there, ask the dangerous question:

*"If I do this, who gets the glory?"*

If David killed Saul, the story would be: "David the Conqueror seized the throne." By sparing Saul, the story became: "God established David's house."

The Inward path brings glory to your layout. The Upward path brings glory to your Lord.

The Audit is the pause. It is the moment you step back from the edge of the cave, put the knife away, and say, *"I will not touch this. I will let God be God."*

# 9

# ALIGN (CALIBRATING TO TRUTH)

You have Arrested the thought ("I want to kill him"). You have Audited the impulse ("I am angry because my ego is threatened"). Now you are sitting in a quiet room with a closed laptop.

The danger is that an empty house gets filled with seven worse demons.

> **Matthew 12:43-45** *"When the unclean spirit has gone out of a person, it passes through waterless places seeking rest, but finds none. Then it says, 'I will return to my house from which I came.' And when it comes, it finds the house empty, swept, and put in order. Then it goes and brings with it seven other spirits more evil than itself... and the last state of that person is worse than the first."*

If you do not fill the void with Truth, the Ego will just rationalize its way back in.

My natural tendency is to shut down when someone pushes back. Rather than exploding, I turn to silence and capitulation. I say "Okay" just to shut the person up. In that silence, I am creating a vacuum. I am not filling the void with Truth; I am filling it with rebellion. I tell myself, "I am just going to do it my way anyway."

I have not aligned with God; I have just gone underground. We need to calibrate the compass before we start moving again.

~

## The Compass vs. The Map

WE ARE OBSESSED with the Map. We want God to tell us *exactly* what to say in the email, which employee to fire, or which city to move to. We want the blue line on the GPS that says, "Turn left in 500 feet."

Why? A Map requires no relationship. You do not need to know the map-maker to follow the blue line. You just need to be obedient. A Map offers certainty. It allows us to be robots who execute a script.

God rarely gives a Map. He gives a Compass.

This confuses us because we think "God's Will" is a destination (The Map). But God's Will is an orientation (The Compass).

- **The Map** tells you *where* to go. (God hides this to build trust).
- **The Compass** tells you *who* to be. (God always reveals this).

A Compass does not tell you where the cliffs are. It does not tell you how to cross the river. It just points North. It says, "This is the direction of Truth. You figure out the terrain."

Alignment is the act of holding your Impulse up against the Compass.

**Impulse:** "I want to crush this employee for their mistake."

**Compass:** "Restore him in a spirit of gentleness." (Galatians 6:1).

**Result:** Misalignment detected. Recalibrating.

~

## The Ventriloquist God

THE PROBLEM IS that we are experts at lying to ourselves. We don't actually want a god; we want a ventriloquist's dummy.

We want a deity that we can put on our lap, throw our voice into, and have it nod along with our bad ideas. We call this "seeking peace," but it is really just "seeking permission."

- We call gossip "venting."
- We call greed "stewardship."
- We call cowardice "keeping the peace."

I used to use the Bible as a weapon against my wife. I would tell her she wasn't a "Proverbs 31 woman" because she wasn't doing what I wanted. I wasn't Aligning with Scripture; I was using Scripture as a club to enforce my will. I was the Ventriloquist, and I made God sound suspiciously like a insecure husband.

To break this delusion, we need something objective. We need a standard that doesn't care about our feelings.

~

## The Three Witnesses

IN A COURT OF LAW, you cannot convict on the testimony of one man. You need witnesses.

> **2 Corinthians 13:1** *"Every charge must be established by the evidence of two or three witnesses."*

When you are about to make a decision, especially one driven by strong emotion, you put your Impulse on trial. You call Three Witnesses to the stand. If they do not agree, you do not move.

### Witness 1: Scripture (The Constitution)

The Bible is the Constitution of the Kingdom. It does not care about your "context." It does not care that your boss is a jerk. It does not care that "everyone else does it."

It is binary. It defines the Standard. We are not looking for a "verse to quote" to win an argument; we are looking for the *character of God* to emulate. Does this decision look like Jesus, or does it look like you?

### Witness 2: Counsel (The Jury)

This is where most leaders fail. We surround ourselves with "Yes Men." We ask friends who will validate us. "Can you believe he said that to me?" "No way, you should definitely fire him." That is not Counsel; that is an echo chamber.

True Counsel often comes from "Balaam's Donkey", the

source you least expect or respect. God often speaks through people we dislike to ensure we are listening to the Message, not the Messenger. Are you looking for *advice* (tell me what to do) or *alignment* (tell me where I am lying to myself)?

**Witness 3: Conscience (The Spirit)**

The Conscience is the internal alarm. It is the "check in the spirit." Be careful: The Conscience is easily seared. If you ignore the alarm enough times, it stops ringing. That is why Conscience is the *third* witness, not the first. It must be calibrated by Scripture and Counsel.

If Scripture + Counsel + Conscience all say "Stop," and you go anyway... that is not a mistake. That is disobedience.

∼

### The $350,000 Lie

I WANT to tell you a story, that I eluded to earlier, about when I violated this. I want to show you what happens when you "Audit" the impulse, see the "Compass," and then decide to walk South anyway.

We had a client who was mis-billed nearly 1,000 hours on a project. Our hourly rate was $350/hour. This wasn't a rounding error; it was a **$350,000 mistake** in our favor.

The client paid it. They didn't catch it. We closed the project. A month later, our accounting team found the error.

**The Impulse:** Keep the money.

**The Rationalization:** Our CFO argued, "If we refund this, we have to lay off two people on your team to cover the shortfall."

This was the perfect trap. It wasn't "Greed vs. Integrity." It was "Loyalty vs. Integrity." The CFO said, "You care about your team, right? You want to protect their jobs?"
I Audited the thought. I knew it was wrong. I Aligned it with the Witnesses.

- **Scripture:** "A false balance is an abomination." (Proverbs 11:1).
- **Conscience:** The alarm was screaming.
- **Counsel:** The CEO sided with the CFO.

I had two Witnesses against one. The Compass pointed North (Refund the money), but I was afraid. I didn't want to fire people. So I became a Ventriloquist. I told myself, "God wants me to protect my team. I am being a 'good shepherd' by hiding this sin."
I stayed quiet. We kept the money. I "saved" the jobs.

≈

### The Cost of Misalignment

YOU CANNOT BUILD a house on a lie. Three months later, the client's auditors found it. They didn't just ask for the money back; they asked *why* we hadn't told them when we found it. We had no answer. We looked incompetent and dishonest.

**The Fallout:**
**We had to refund the money anyway.**

- **The "Job Protection" excuse evaporated.** We still had the budget hole.
- **We lost the client.** They fired us. We lost millions in future revenue.
- **I lost my authority.** When I spoke to my team about "integrity," my words tasted like ash.

I tried to save the map (the jobs) by breaking the compass (the truth). I lost both. Scripture isn't a suggestion.

**Numbers 32:23** *"Be sure your sin will find you out."*

Not "might." *Will.* It is inevitable. You can rationalize, you can justify, you can play the Ventriloquist, but you cannot mock God.

Alignment is not about being perfect. It is about being honest. It is about looking at the Compass, seeing you are headed South, and having the courage to turn the ship around, especially when it costs you $350,000, because the alternative costs you your soul.

## 10

## ACT (MOVING IN FAITH)

You have Arrested the thought. You have Audited the impulse. You have Aligned with Truth and know exactly what you *should* do. Now comes the hardest part. Doing it!

You absolutely do not want to do it. Every fiber of your flesh is screaming "No." You feel resistance. You feel tired. You feel humiliated. The clarity of the Alignment phase has faded, and now you are staring at a concrete action that feels like death.

We often call this "hypocrisy." We think, "If I do this good thing while feeling this bad way, I am being a fake. I am just acting."

We have it backward. This is not hypocrisy; it is **Discipline.** Hypocrisy is concealing sin to look righteous. Discipline is acting *against* the impulse of sin to achieve righteousness.

Faith is not a feeling you wait for; it is a movement you initiate. You act your way into a new feeling; you rarely feel your way into a new action.

∾

## The Charity Event Disaster

I REMEMBER LEADING a men's event last year. We were organizing a massive event, our largest ever. On the flyer, it looked inspiring. It was titled "The Father Heart of God" and was aimed at men with troubled childhoods. We had a great band lined up for worship. We had local businesses sponsoring. The reality of the event was a nightmare.

Two days before, three key volunteers bailed. The food order was wrong. The caterer thought we needed snacks for 50, not lunch for 150, and our worship center did not have enough tables to seat the men comfortably.

I was driving to the venue at 7:00 AM on a Saturday to set up tables. I was not humming worship songs. I was angry. I was resentful. I was tired. I thought, "I am a fraud. I am about to speak at this event about being a man of God and good husband and father, and I want to yell at the caterer. I do not want to be here. I want to be home on my couch."

I felt distant from God. I felt like a "fake" leader because my heart was not "in it." I had a choice. I could follow my feelings and probably ruin the event (or show up with a toxic attitude), or I could follow the Protocol.

**The Act** was not the event itself. The Act was sending the polite text to the caterer when I wanted to scream. The Act was walking into the worship center and setting up 150 chairs and tables knowing it was going to be uncomfortable. The Act was shaking hands with the first guy who walked in and smiling, even though I felt dead inside, and then, something happened.

The event started. The worship began. The men started

arriving. I saw a single man walk in, looking exhausted, and leave with a renewed vigor for the Lord. I saw neighbors laughing and eating together. Suddenly, my tank was full. I felt close to God. The resentment evaporated, replaced by a deep sense of purpose and joy.

I realized something profound that day: **The feeling of closeness was the *reward* for obedience, not the *fuel* for it.**

$\sim$

### Kinetic Faith

THERE IS a principle in physics called friction. **Static friction** is the force that keeps a stationary object from moving. **Kinetic friction** is the force that resists an object that is already moving.

Static friction is always higher than kinetic friction. It takes more force to *start* pushing a heavy box than it does to *keep* it moving.

The same is true in the Spirit. The hardest part of the "Act" is the first 30 seconds.

We often wait for the feeling of faith to hit us before we move. We want the "peace" to wash over us. We want the excitement to propel us, but God often works in reverse.

**Joshua 3:15-16** *"Now the Jordan is at flood stage all during harvest. Yet as soon as the priests who carried the ark reached the Jordan and their feet touched the water's edge, the water from upstream stopped flowing."*

The priests had to step into the river *while it was still flooding*. The water did not part when they prayed. It did not part when they Aligned. It parted when their feet got wet.

God often waits for your foot to hit the water before He moves the river. He gives the impulse to move, but you must provide the motion. If you wait for dry ground, for feelings of safety, peace, or excitement, you will die on the bank.

~

## Obedience in the Dark

THERE ARE times when the lights go out. In Chapter 1, we talked about the Silence. In Chapter 2, we talked about the lack of signs. Sometimes, you are in a season where you feel nothing but your own exhaustion. This is "The Dark."

Obedience in the light is easy. When the blessings are flowing, the team is winning, and the profits are up, it is easy to say, "God is good" and act with integrity.

Obedience in the dark is the true test of leadership.

- A servant works when the Master is watching.
- A son works because he owns the outcome.

Doing the right thing when you feel "dead" inside is not a sign of spiritual coldness. It is a sign of spiritual maturity. It proves you serve the God of the work, not just the "high" of the work.

~

## The Tuesday Afternoon Test

LET us go back to the office. It is Tuesday at 2:00 PM.

You just had a heated exchange with a peer in a strategy meeting. You disrespected them in front of the team. You made a sarcastic comment that got a laugh but crushed their spirit. You go back to your office.

1. **ARREST:** You stop the momentum. You realize you are still fuming, replaying the argument. You stop the train.
2. **AUDIT:** You ask, "Why am I angry?" You realize it was not about the strategy; it was about your Ego. They challenged your authority, and you snapped.
3. **ALIGN:** You check the Compass. Scripture says, *"If you are offering your gift at the altar and there remember that your brother has something against you, leave your gift there... First go and be reconciled to your brother"* (Matthew 5:23-24).
4. **ACT:** You know what you need to do. You need to go to their office and apologize, but you do not want to. You feel the resistance. You feel the humiliation. Your brain starts offering alternatives: "I will just send a text." "I will do it tomorrow." "They started it anyway."

This is the Hypocrisy Gap. You do not *feel* sorry yet. You still feel annoyed.

**The Act:** You physically stand up. You walk down the hall. You knock on the door. You open your mouth.

"Hey, I was out of line in that meeting. I let my ego get the better of me, and I disrespected you. I am sorry. Will you forgive me?"

You do not wait to "feel" the apology. You speak the words because they are True.

**The Result:** The tension breaks. They likely soften. The relationship is healed, and usually, about 10 minutes later, your feelings catch up. You feel the relief and the peace of righteousness.

~

### Closing the Loop

THIS IS THE PROTOCOL.

- **ARREST:** Stop the train. (Authority).
- **AUDIT:** Check the cargo. (Interrogation).
- **ALIGN:** Check the map. (Standard).
- **ACT:** Move the feet. (Execution).

If you run this loop consistently, you stop being a slave to your impulses. You stop being a leader who is tossed back and forth by waves of emotion or pressure. You start becoming a leader who is governed by God. You have the Tools. Now we need to apply it.

In the next section of the book, we are going to look at the three biggest areas where leaders fail, and how to construct the structural defenses that keep us standing. We are moving from the Protocol to The Fortress.

# PART III

# CONSTRUCTING THE FORTRESS

A protocol is useless if it stays in the abstract. A blueprint provides no protection if it stays on the paper. It must be built. It must be constructed in the real world, amidst the real pressures and problems we face every day.

In this section, we take the Watchman's Protocol (Arrest, Audit, Align, Act) and use it to construct the three essential components of a leader's life.

**The Integrity Foundation** challenges us to govern our "Yes" and our "No." It reveals how the catastrophic moral collapses we see in leadership are rarely sudden accidents; they are structural failures caused by a thousand tiny hairline fractures in the concrete. We will learn how small honesties cure the foundation that holds up everything else.

**The Emotional Walls** teach us how to create a safe container for the inevitable frustration, disappointment, and loneliness of leadership. We often think our only options are to suppress our emotions (no walls) or to be ruled by them (broken walls). There is a third way: processing them within the Fortress with God. We will learn to bring our raw, unfiltered emotions to Him, allowing the walls to hold the chaos while He metabolizes our pain into wisdom.

**The Relational Gates** focus on how we govern access— what we let in and what we let out. As leaders, our words carry weight. We can use them to reinforce the gate or to burn it down. We will explore how to protect our teams, our families, and our reputation by applying the Protocol to our tongue and our tone.

This is where the blueprints become the building. This is where theory becomes practice. This is where we learn to live out our leadership not just in the boardroom, but in the quiet, unseen moments that define who we truly are.

# 11

# THE INTEGRITY FOUNDATION

I told you about the $350,000 billing error. I told you how I caved to pressure, kept the money, and eventually lost the client and my integrity.

For years, I looked back on that moment as a singular failure of courage. I thought, "The pressure was just too high in that room. If I had just been stronger in that moment, I would have passed the test." I was wrong.

I recently did an autopsy on that collapse. I realized that I did not fail because the pressure was high. I failed because my **Integrity Foundation** was too shallow. You do not become a liar the day you sign a fraudulent contract. You become a liar the day you lie about why you were late to a meeting.

Looking back, the collapse started years before. It started when I told a client, "We are almost done," when I had not even started. It started when I told my wife, "I am leaving the office now," when I was still typing an email. It started when I expensed a personal lunch because "the company owes me."

The big collapse is just the final receipt for a thousand small compromises.

~

## Structural Integrity

IN ENGINEERING, "INTEGRITY" does not mean "moral goodness." It means the structure is whole. It is undivided. A building with structural integrity holds up under load. A building with micro-fractures collapses when the wind blows.

We tend to view integrity as a character trait, something you either have or you do not. "He is a man of integrity," integrity is not a trait. It is a **Stack**.

Imagine your character is a wall. Every time you tell the truth when it is awkward, you add a steel beam to the stack. Every time you admit a mistake when you could have blamed a vendor, you pour concrete.

Every time you exaggerate a metric to look good, you remove a bolt. Every time you say "I am fine" when you are dying inside, you create a hairline fracture. We think the "little white lies" do not count. We think, "I am just managing perceptions. I am just buying time."

The little lies are the *only* ones that count. They are the ones that train your reflex. They teach your nervous system that Truth is negotiable.

∿

## Governing the "Yes" and "No"

**Matthew 5:37** *"Let what you say be simply 'Yes' or 'No'; anything more than this comes from evil."*

JESUS IS NOT JUST BEING a strict moralist here. He is giving us the blueprint for authority. The translation is simple: Stop spinning. Stop managing perceptions. Just state reality.

The most common failure mode for leaders is not the bold-faced lie. It is the **Strategic Exaggeration**.

- "I will have it to you by end of day." (You know you will not).
- "The traffic was bad." (You left 10 minutes late).
- "It is in final review." (You have not opened the file).

When you use words to manipulate reality rather than describe it, you erode your own authority. You teach your own soul that your word is hollow.

∿

## Applying the Protocol

LET us put this into the Protocol.

**The Scenario:** You are in a status meeting with your boss. You have not done the task you promised. The boss asks, "Where are we on the Q3 report?"

**The Impulse:** "It is coming along great. Just polishing up a few details. I will have it to you shortly." This is a lie. It is a protective shield designed to deflect shame and buy time.

**ARREST:** You feel the heat in your face. You feel the impulse to spin. You stop the mouth. You do not let the lie escape.

**AUDIT:** Why do I want to lie?

- *Fear:* I do not want to look incompetent.
- *Pride:* I do not want to admit I dropped the ball.

**ALIGN:** What is the standard?

- *Truth:* "Lying lips are an abomination" (Proverbs 12:22).
- *Reality:* If I lie, I have to remember the lie. I have to create a fake timeline. If I tell the truth, I am free.

**ACT:** Speak the hard truth. "I missed it. I have not started. I completely dropped the ball. I will have it to you by tomorrow morning."

**The Result:** You take a hit. Your ego bruises. Your boss might be annoyed, but you added a massive brick to your **Integrity Foundation.** You are stewarding the grace of truth. You have proven to yourself that you fear God (Truth) more than you fear man (Disapproval).

～

## The Theology: Truth as Reality

TRUTH IS NOT JUST a rule in a book. Truth is the nature of Reality itself. God *is* Truth. When you align with Truth, you align with how the universe actually works. You are building on rock.

When you lie, you are trying to create a false reality. You are trying to build a world where you did not miss the deadline, or where you did not make the mistake. You are trying to play God.

This is the **Daniel Principle**. Daniel did not start his career by facing lions. He started by refusing the King's food (Daniel 1). It was a small thing. A dietary preference, but he drew a line.

He held the line on the menu, he had the strength to hold the line on the worship (Daniel 6). You cannot survive the Lion's Den if you have not survived the King's Table.

～

## The Tuesday Afternoon Test

HERE IS your test for this week. It is the **Expense Report**.

You took a client to lunch. It was $48. You tip $12 to make it an even $60, but you also bought a $4 coffee for yourself on the way back. Do you lump it in?

"It is just $4. The company makes millions. They owe me for all the overtime I work."

It is not about the money. It is about the **Fortress**. If you can be bought for $4, you can be bought for $350,000. The price is different, but the principle is the same. You are selling your integrity for a benefit.

**The Call:** Find one area where you are "managing perception" instead of telling the truth.

- Maybe it is your time sheet.
- Maybe it is how you talk to your spouse about money.
- Maybe it is the reason you gave for cancelling a meeting.

Arrest it today. Correct the record.

"Hey, I said I was stuck in traffic. Actually, I just left late. Sorry for the inaccuracy."

It will feel awkward. It will feel like death to your ego, but it will bring life to your soul.

# 12

# THE EMOTIONAL WALLS

There is a pervasive myth in leadership circles, especially Christian ones. It is the Myth of the Robot Leader. We believe that the best leaders are emotionless. We look at the stoic CEO who never flinches, or the pastor who never seems rattled, and we think, "That is strength." We confuse "composure" with "numbness."

You were designed to feel. God feels. Scripture tells us He feels anger, grief, joy, and jealousy. To kill your emotions is to kill the *Imago Dei*, the Image of God, in you.

The danger is that emotions that are ignored do not die; they are buried alive. They resurface as burnout, cynicism, or a heart attack at 45. You do not need to feel *less* to lead well; you need to govern *more*. Emotions are data, not directives.

∽

## The Fork in the Road: Suppression vs. Surrender

WHEN THE PRESSURE HITS, you have two options.

OPTION 1: **The Stoic (Suppression)** This is the default for most men. You grit your teeth. You say, "I am fine." You say, "It is what it is." You push the anger down into your gut.

The result is "The Leak." You hold it together at work, but you snap at your wife over the dishwasher. You are sarcastic with your kids. You self-medicate (food, drink, screens, or worse) to numb the pressure.

OPTION 2: **The Christian (Surrender)** This is the path of the **Emotional Walls.** You acknowledge the reality before God. You say, "I am angry." "I am disappointed." "I feel betrayed." The result is that the pressure valve is released *upward*, not *outward*.

∽

## The Tool: Lament (Complaining Upward)

WE HAVE LOST the art of Lament. We think it is unspiritual to complain to God, but Lament is not whining. Whining is complaining to people who cannot fix it. Lament is bringing the raw, unfiltered mess to the One who can handle it.

Over one-third of the Psalms are laments.

**Psalm 13:1** *"How long, O Lord? Will you forget me forever?"*

David did not "clean up" his emotions before praying. He did not put on his "Sunday best" voice. He prayed *through* the mess.

You cannot govern an emotion you refuse to name.

1. **Name it:** "I feel betrayed."
2. **Speak it to God:** "Lord, this sucks. I want to quit. I am angry at You for letting this happen."
3. **Leave it there:** "I trust in your unfailing love."

∼

### Applying the Protocol

LET us go back to that Men's Ministry event from Chapter 7. We talked about the logistics, the chairs, the caterer. Let us talk about the **Emotional Reality**.

It is 48 hours before the event. I get a text from my key volunteer: "Hey man, something came up. Cannot make it." He did not even call. He sent a text.

I felt a surge of anger. I wanted to text him back: "Are you kidding me? You are leaving us high and dry." I wanted to snap back with witty remarks that were cutting.

**ARREST:** I stopped the text. I stopped the spiral of "I am never doing this again." I physically put the phone down.

**AUDIT:** What am I feeling?

- *Frustration:* Yes. He flaked.
- *Fear:* Yes. I am afraid the event will fail and I will look like an idiot.
- *Fatigue:* Yes. I am tired of carrying this alone.

**ALIGN:** What is true?

- *Standard:* "Be angry and do not sin" (Ephesians 4:26). I can feel the anger without acting on it.
- *Truth:* People are unreliable at times. God is faithful and always reliable! My identity is not in this event's logistics.

**ACT:** I picked up the phone. I did not text; I called. I left a voicemail. "Hey man, we will miss you. Hope everything is okay. We will figure it out."

Then I went to the venue and set up the chairs. I did the work while feeling the weight. I did not pretend I was happy. I just did the job.

~

### The Tuesday Afternoon Test

HERE IS a scenario that breaks many leaders. You pour six months of your life into a project. You build the team. You build the prototype. You work late nights. You believe in it.

Then, on a Tuesday afternoon, you get an email from Corporate. "Strategic pivot. Project cancelled. Stop all work immediately." You are devastated. You feel wasted. You feel like a pawn.

**The Test:** How do you lead your team the next morning?

**Bad Leadership:** You vent to the team. "Corporate are idiots. They do not know what they are doing. I cannot believe this."

*Result:* You poison the culture. You create an "Us vs. Them" mentality.

**Stoic Leadership:** You walk in with a stone face. "Business is business. We pivot. Next project."

*Result:* You create a cold culture. Your team feels unheard and unvalued.

**Governed Leadership:** You process the grief with God first. You Lament. You scream in your car on the way to work. You get the poison out.
Then, you walk into the room. "Guys, this is hard. I am disappointed too. We poured a lot into this, and it hurts to see it go. Take a moment to grieve it, but here is the reality: We learned a lot. We built a great team, and now we are going to apply that to the next mission."

**The Win:** You validate the team's emotion because you have processed your own. You become a "safe container" for their chaos.

~

### Jesus Wept

**John 11:35** *"Jesus wept."*

IT IS the shortest verse in the Bible, and one of the most profound. Jesus knew He was about to raise Lazarus from the dead. He knew the outcome was victory. He knew that in 10 minutes, everyone would be cheering.

He *still* stopped to feel the grief of the moment. He didn't rush past the pain to get to the miracle. Efficiency is not the highest good. Humanity is.

A leader who cannot weep cannot lead people; they can only manage resources. Your Emotional **Walls** allow you to be present with people in their pain without being overwhelmed by it.

## 13

# THE RELATIONAL GATES

As you rise in leadership, your words gain mass. When a junior developer makes a suggestion, it is a suggestion. When the CTO makes a suggestion, it is a mandate. When a peer makes a sarcastic joke, it is annoying. When a leader makes a sarcastic joke, it is a wound.

I remember a moment early in my leadership career. We were in a design review. A young designer presented a concept that I thought was cluttered. I did not say, "I think this is cluttered." I said, "Wow, did we get paid by the pixel for this one?"

The room chuckled. I felt witty. I moved on. Three years later, that designer told me, "I almost quit that day. You made me feel like an idiot in front of the whole team."

I did not even remember saying it. It was a throwaway comment to me, but to him, it was a crushing weight.

You cannot lead people if you cannot govern your mouth. An ungoverned tongue does not just create awkward moments; it creates unsafe cultures.

~

## The Rudder and The Fire

**James 3:4-5** *"Look at the ships also: though they are so large and are driven by strong winds, they are guided by a very small rudder wherever the will of the pilot directs. So also the tongue is a small member, yet it boasts of great things. How great a forest is set ablaze by such a small fire!"*

JAMES GIVES US TWO METAPHORS: The Rudder and The Fire.

**The Rudder:** Your entire organizational culture is steered by your small comments. If you are cynical, the ship steers toward cynicism. If you are encouraging, the ship steers toward hope.

**The Fire:** A small spark sets a forest ablaze. One "venting" session with a manager can burn down trust that took three years to build.

Relational equity is stacked slowly and burned quickly.

- Every encouraging word is a deposit.
- Every cynical remark is a withdrawal.

**Key Insight:** You are usually overdrawn without knowing it.

~

## The Danger: Sarcasm and "Just Joking"

SMART PEOPLE ARE OFTEN SARCASTIC. It feels like wit. It feels like "keeping it real." We pride ourselves on our ability to have a "sharp tongue," but the word sarcasm comes from the Greek *sarkazein*, which literally means "to tear flesh."

Sarcasm is hostility disguised as humor. It is a way to say the hard thing without taking responsibility for it. "I was just joking!" is the coward's defense.

**The Audit:** When you use sarcasm, what are you protecting? Usually, you are too cowardly to say the hard thing directly, so you say it sideways to protect yourself while cutting them. Governing your tongue means killing the "cheap shot" to preserve the relationship.

~

## Applying the Protocol

THE SCENARIO: You are in a project review. A team member has submitted a draft that ignores the core requirements you agreed on. It is a mess.

**The Impulse:** "Did you even read the requirements? This is a disaster."

**ARREST:** Bite your tongue. Literally. Do not let the shaming comment escape. Feel the heat of your impatience.

**AUDIT:** Why do I want to shame them?

- *Ego:* I want to show everyone how smart I am by highlighting how dumb they are.
- *Impatience:* I just want this done, and their incompetence is slowing me down.

**ALIGN:** What is the goal?

- *Standard:* "Let no corrupting talk come out of your mouths, but only such as is good for building up" (Ephesians 4:29).
- *Goal:* Correction, not destruction. I want her to do better work, not to feel like garbage.

**ACT:** Ask a guiding question. "Help me understand the logic here. How does this handle the scale issue we discussed?"

∾

### Protection from YOU

IN MY FIRST BOOK, Christian Leadership in the Professional World, we talked about "Protection" as the duty of a leader to defend the team from toxic clients, unreasonable deadlines, and corporate politics. In this book, we have to face a harder truth.

If you lack self-governance, **YOU** are the threat the team needs protection from.

- If you are moody, they walk on eggshells.
- If you are reactive, they hide bad news.
- If you are ungoverned, you create the very toxicity you claim to hate.

When you govern yourself, you become a "Safe Place." People bring you their best work and their hardest problems because they know they will not get burned by your lack of discipline.

～

### The Tuesday Afternoon Test

IT IS 2:30 PM. You get a Slack message from a peer that misunderstands your project and accuses your team of dropping the ball. You start typing. The keys are clacking loud. You are drafting a "nastygram." You are cc'ing their boss. You are bringing the receipts.

**The Test:** Stop. Read it out loud.

- Is it necessary?
- Is it kind?
- Does it need to be public?

**The Action:** Delete the draft. Do not hit send.
Pick up the phone or walk to their desk. "Hey, I saw your message. I think there is a disconnect. Do you have five minutes to walk through the logic? I need to understand this more."

**The Result:** You saved their dignity. You saved your authority. You reinforced the **Relational Gate.**

~

### Transition

WE HAVE BUILT THE PROTOCOL. We have applied it to Integrity, Emotion, and Relationships. We have moved from the internal work of the leader to the external impact on the team.

What happens when you actually live this way? What happens when you **cement** these decisions for 5, 10, or 20 years?

You become something rare. You become a **Stronghold.**

In the final section of this book, we will look at the Fruit of the Will of God.

# PART IV

# THE FRUIT

What does a leader look like who has walked through the Silence, mastered the Protocol, and **built their Fortress** on the Rock? They look like a **Stronghold**.

In a world of reactive, fearful, and exhausted leaders, the one who leads from a place of deep rest is a radical anomaly. This is not about personality; it is about proximity. It is about being so close to the Father that the chaos of the world cannot shake you.

We will contrast the leadership of Saul (insecure, people-pleasing, and ultimately destructive) with the leadership of David (flawed, yet a man after God's own heart). We will see that the difference wasn't skill or talent; it was the source of their strength.

Finally, we will conclude by looking at the parable of the wise and foolish builders. The storm comes to everyone. The rain falls on the just and the unjust. The difference is not the storm; the difference is the foundation.

The work we do in the dark, the wrestling in the Silence,

the discipline of the Protocol, the **laying** of small obedi-ences, is what builds the foundation. It is what ensures that when the winds blow and the floods rise, the house will stand.

This is the fruit of the work. This is Christian Leader-ship in the Silence.

## 14

## THE STRONGHOLD

I t is 3:00 PM on a Friday. A junior engineer runs into your office, face pale, hands shaking.

"I think I just deleted the production database."

For the non-techies: The production database is the master record of everything the company owns. Deleting it is like burning down the library. The revenue target is missed. The client lawsuit is looming. The crisis is here.

I have seen two types of leaders in this moment.

LEADER A (THE RUIN): They scream. They pace the room. Their eyes go wide. They start blaming. *"How could you be so stupid? Do you know what this costs us?"* They radiate a frequency that says, *We are doomed.*

Why do they panic? They have no walls. The chaos of the external world walks right into their internal world. They are exposed.

.   .   .

LEADER B (THE STRONGHOLD): They sit down. They lower the volume of their voice. They look the engineer in the eye and say, "Okay. Breathe. Tell me exactly what happened. We will solve this." They radiate a frequency that says, We will survive.

The principle is simple: **Anxiety is contagious, but so is peace.** If the pilot is panicked, the passengers riot. If the pilot is calm, the passengers trust.

You cannot demand a calm culture if you bring a chaotic spirit. Your team regulates their nervous system off of yours.

~

### Becoming the Stronghold

EDWIN FRIEDMAN COINED the term "Non-Anxious Presence." In the context of our Fortress, this means **Structural Integrity.**

It does not mean "lack of caring." It is not apathy. It is lack of reactivity. It means you are separate from the chaos around you. You can be *in* the storm without letting the storm get *in* you.

This is the fruit of the construction work we have been doing.

- You are not anxious about the lie being found out; you have built the **Integrity Foundation.**
- You are not overwhelmed by the anger; you have built the **Emotional Walls.**
- You do not need to destroy people to feel safe; you have manned the **Relational Gates.**

The Fortress creates the sanctuary where wisdom can exist, even when the world is burning down outside.

~

## Saul vs. David: The Tent and the Tower

THE BIBLE GIVES us a perfect case study in 1 Samuel.

SAUL IS THE TENT. He is unfortified. He is insecure. He is reactive. When the pressure mounts, he collapses. When he feels threatened by David's success, he throws a spear at him.

> *1 Samuel 18:11 "And Saul hurled the spear, for he thought, 'I will pin David to the wall.' But David evaded him twice."*

Why did Saul throw the spear? He had no internal walls to contain his fear. He needed to control David because he could not control Saul.

DAVID IS THE FORTRESS. He is secure. When Saul throws the spear, David does not throw it back. He dodges it.

An ungoverned leader (The Tent) tries to control everyone else to quiet their own internal noise. A governed leader (The Fortress) does not need to control others because their internal world is settled.

Consider Abigail in 1 Samuel 25. Her husband, Nabal, was a fool who insulted David. David lost his cool and marched 400 men to slaughter the household.

Abigail rode out to meet the army. She did not panic. She brought food, bowed low, and spoke with such profound wisdom that she de-escalated a massacre.

She was a **Stronghold** in the middle of a war zone. She

saved her family not by fighting, but by governing herself when powerful men were losing their minds.

≈

## Leading from a Full Tank

REMEMBER the Men's Event from Chapter 8? I told you about the moment I felt God's pleasure; a full tank of spiritual satisfaction. That fullness did not come from the event's success. It came from the obedience in the dark.

When you lead from within the Fortress:

- You do not need the team to validate you.
- You do not need the "win" to prove your foundation is solid.
- You do not need the subordinate to agree with you to feel safe.

This makes you dangerous to the enemy and safe for your people.

≈

## The Peace That Garrisons the Heart

*Philippians 4:7 "And the peace of God, which surpasses all understanding, will guard your hearts and your minds in Christ Jesus."*

NOTICE THE WORD **GUARD**. It is a military term (*phroureō*). It means to mount a garrison. To station a sentinel.

The peace of God is not a soft blanket. It is an armed Sentry standing at the Gate of your Fortress.

It stops the panic from entering. It surpasses understanding because it does not make logical sense.

- The metrics say "Panic."
- The board says "Fear."
- The Watchman says "Peace."

This peace is not a mental trick. It is the result of knowing who holds the Blueprints.

~

### The Tuesday Afternoon Test: The Shelter

HERE IS the hardest test of all. Layoffs are coming. The budget has been cut. The team is scared. Rumors are flying on Slack.

THE ANXIOUS LEADER **(The Ruin)** hides in their office. They give vague answers. They snap at people asking questions because they are terrified of the conflict. They create more fear.

THE ALIGNED LEADER **(The Fortress)** calls a meeting. They stand in front of the room. They don't smile fake smiles.

*"I know you are scared. I cannot tell you everything yet, but I will tell you the truth as soon as I can. We are going to walk through this together."*

The bad news did not change. The storm is still raging, but the **Fortress** they are standing in did change.

The team feels held, not abandoned. They feel sheltered. You built the walls on a quiet Tuesday, you can offer them safety on a chaotic Friday.

You have stopped the momentum. You have built the Fortress. You have become the Stronghold for them, through Christ, but will it hold against the hurricane?

When the real storm hits, the cancer diagnosis, the bankruptcy, the total betrayal, will this foundation actually work?

In the final chapter, we will inspect the rock.

# 15

# WHAT YOU LEAVE STANDING

L eadership is temporary. Titles change. Roles end. Offices empty. Eventually, every leader leaves the room. The real question is not how powerful you were while you were present. The real question is **what remains when you are gone.**

A governed leader leaves behind more than results. They leave behind structure.

~

### The Myth of the Indispensable Leader

INSECURE LEADERS TRY to make themselves irreplaceable. They hoard decisions. They centralize authority. They believe everything will fall apart without them.

This feels like importance. It is actually fragility. A leader who must always be present has built a personality, not a fortress. When they leave, confusion rushes in to fill the vacuum.

~

## What Strongholds Create

A STRONGHOLD DOES SOMETHING DIFFERENT. It stabilizes people.

It clarifies expectations. It trains judgment.

Under a governed leader:

- Decisions get better, not just faster
- Conflict is addressed, not avoided
- Truth becomes normal, not heroic

The team doesn't need constant supervision because the **walls are internalized.** That is legacy.

~

## Culture Is a Residue

CULTURE IS NOT what you say in all-hands meetings. Culture is what people default to when no one is watching.

Your reactions train reactions. Your silences train silence. Your integrity trains integrity. Over time, your leadership leaves fingerprints everywhere. You don't get to opt out of this. You only get to choose whether the imprint is intentional.

~

### Saul Builds Dependence. David Builds Strength.

SAUL NEEDED people to need him. When he felt threatened, he tightened control. When he felt exposed, he lashed out. His leadership produced fear and fragility.

David built something sturdier. Even when David failed morally, the structure held. Men like Nathan could confront him. Women like Abigail could speak wisdom into chaos. The kingdom endured.

David's strength was not perfection. It was **governance.**

~

### What Happens After You Leave

A REVEALING QUESTION for any leader: *What happens when you take a week off?*

- If everything stalls, you've built dependency.
- If everything collapses, you've built fear.
- If things continue with clarity and steadiness, you've built a fortress.

Strong leadership reproduces strength. Weak leadership reproduces chaos.

~

### The Long View of Obedience

MOST OF THE fruit of governed leadership appears late. You rarely see it in quarterly reports.

You see it in:

- Teams that tell the truth without fear
- Leaders who admit mistakes early
- Cultures that recover quickly from stress

This is compound obedience. One small decision at a time. One arrested impulse. One repaired breach. One aligned action. Over years, it becomes unmistakable.

∿

## You Are Training Your Replacement

EVERY LEADER IS TRAINING their replacement, whether they mean to or not.

- Your habits become permission structures.
- Your standards become norms.
- Your Protocol becomes the unwritten law.

The goal is not to be remembered. The goal is to be **missed as little as possible.** What you built can stand on its own.

∿

## The Quiet Success

THE HIGHEST COMPLIMENT a leader can receive is rarely spoken to them. It sounds like this, said years later: "We learned how to lead because of how they led us." No applause. No monument. Just strength that remains.

THAT IS FRUIT THAT LASTS.

## 16

# REPAIRING THE BREACH

Y ou are going to fail. I wish I could tell you that reading this book, memorizing the Protocol, and building your Fortress will make you immune to failure. It won't.

You will have days where the Watchman falls asleep at the gate. You will have moments where the pressure is too high, and your Emotional Walls buckle. You will have Tuesday afternoons where you are tired and weak, and you lay a brick of compromise instead of a brick of discipline.

You will snap at your spouse. You will shade the truth in a meeting. You will let your ego drive the car.

The enemy of your soul does not need to destroy the entire fortress to win. He just needs you to believe that **one crack means the whole thing is ruined.**

When we fail, the immediate temptation is abandonment. We think: *"I messed up. I'm a hypocrite. I tried this 'Decision Fortress' thing and I still lost my temper. I might as well give up."*

We look at the breach in the wall and we walk away from the gate. **This is a lie.**

∽

**A breach is not a demolition. It is a repair order.**

THE NEHEMIAH PRINCIPLE

In the book of Nehemiah, the walls of Jerusalem were broken down. They were piles of rubble. The gates were burned with fire. The people were living in shame, exposed to their enemies.

Nehemiah did not look at the ruin and say, "Well, it's over. God has left."

He looked at the ruin and said:

Nehemiah 2:17 *"Come, let us rebuild the wall of Jerusalem, and we will no longer be in disgrace."*

He didn't build a *new* wall. He repaired the *old* one. He used the foundation that was already there.

In leadership, resilience is not about never failing. It is about how quickly you mix the mortar when a brick falls out.

∽

**The Repair Protocol**

WHEN YOU FAIL, when you violate your own standards, you need a protocol for repair. You cannot just "try harder" next time. You have to fix the breach before you can return to the watch.

.　.　.

1. **OWN THE RUIN (The Audit)** When a wall cracks, the worst thing you can do is paint over it. Structural failure cannot be hidden; it must be exposed.

When you snap at your team or lie about a deadline, do not rationalize it. Do not say, *"I was tired,"* or *"They provoked me."* That is painting over the crack.

Stand in front of the breach and admit it. *"I failed. I lost my temper. I lied. This is a hole in my wall."*

2. **CLEAR THE RUBBLE (Confession)** You cannot lay fresh bricks on top of loose debris. You have to clear the site.

In the spiritual life, debris is **unconfessed sin**. It is the shame and the excuses you pile on top of the failure.

- **Vertical Confession:** Go to God. *"Lord, I abandoned my post. I let the enemy in. Forgive me."*
- **Horizontal Confession:** Go to the people you hurt. *"I was wrong. I spoke to you disrespectfully. There is no excuse. Will you forgive me?"*

Clearing the rubble hurts. It is humbling, but it clears the way for new construction.

3. **LAY THE FRESH BRICK (Repentance)** Confession is saying "I was wrong." Repentance is fixing the wall.

If you lied, the repair isn't just saying sorry; it is telling the truth. If you stole credit, the repair isn't just apologizing; it is publicly giving the credit to the right person.

You must do the **next right thing** immediately. Do not wait for the feeling of "holiness" to return. Pick up the trowel and lay the brick of obedience right where the brick of compromise used to be.

**4. SET A DOUBLE GUARD (Accountability)** In Nehemiah 4, when the enemies threatened to attack the weak spots, Nehemiah didn't just hope for the best. He posted a guard *day and night*.

If you failed in your integrity, you have a weak spot in the wall. You cannot trust yourself there right now. You need a second Watchman.

Tell a friend. Tell your spouse. *"I am struggling with this specific area. I need you to stand on the wall with me for a while."*

～

### The Sword and the Trowel

Nehemiah 4:17 *"Those who carried burdens were loaded in such a way that each labored on the work with one hand and held his weapon with the other."*

THIS IS the picture of the recovering leader. You have a **trowel** in one hand, building, repairing, doing the work. You have a **sword** in the other, fighting off the shame that tells you to quit.

The enemy wants you to look at the breach and define yourself by it. *"You are a liar. You are a failure. You are an angry man."*

The Watchman looks at the breach and defines himself by the repair. *"I am a builder, and today, I am fixing this hole."*

~

## Do Not Abandon the Gate

THE MOST DANGEROUS moment in your leadership is not the moment you sin. It is the moment *after* you sin.

That is the moment you decide whether to let the breach become a gateway for the enemy, or a monument to God's grace.

If you have failed, get up. If you have cracked, repair it. If you have fallen asleep, wake up.

The Fortress is not built by perfect people. It is built by people who know how to use a trowel. Clear the rubble. Fix the breach.


GET BACK ON THE WALL.

# 17

# MY STANDING ORDERS

Every fortress runs on standing orders. Standing orders are decisions you make *once* so you don't have to make them again under pressure. They are the rules you don't renegotiate when you're tired, emotional, or afraid.

I didn't write these because I'm disciplined. I wrote them because I'm not. Left to myself, I drift. I rationalize. I get quiet when I should speak and sharp when I should listen. These orders exist to govern *me* before I try to govern anyone else. They are not aspirational. They are protective.

∽

### Order 1: I Do Not Lie to Protect Myself

I DON'T SPIN. I don't shade. I don't "buy time" with half-truths. If I miss a deadline, I say I missed it. If I make a mistake, I own it. If I don't know, I say I don't know.

This order exists because I know how easily fear turns into deception. One lie never stays alone. It demands more bricks of compromise to hold it up. Truth is slower. Truth hurts more. Truth always builds a stronger foundation.

~

## Order 2: I Do Not Lead While Physiologically Compromised

IF I AM H.A.L.T. (HUNGRY, angry, lonely, or tired) I do not make high-impact decisions. I don't send the email. I don't fire the shot. I don't "clear the air." I eat. I rest. I take a walk.

This isn't weakness. It's stewardship. Exhaustion makes cowards of us all, and I refuse to let biology masquerade as wisdom.

~

## Order 3: I Never Send Important Messages at Night

NIGHT IS where good intentions go to die. If something feels urgent after 9 PM, it almost never is. It's usually fatigue dressed as conviction.

Emails written at night are rewritten in the morning, or deleted entirely. Conversations started late are postponed until clarity returns. Darkness distorts perspective. I don't trust it.

∿

## Order 4: I Do Not Vent Downward

I DO NOT UNLOAD my frustration on people who can't fight back. My team is not my therapy group. My family is not my pressure valve.

If I'm angry, I take it upward, to God, to my wife, or to a peer who has permission to challenge me. Leaders who vent downward poison the well they drink from.

∿

## Order 5: I Move Toward Conflict, Not Around It

AVOIDANCE FEELS PEACEFUL. It is not. If something is unresolved, I don't let it rot. I don't triangulate. I don't hope it "resolves itself." I go to the person. I tell the truth plainly. I listen without preparing my defense.

Conflict avoided becomes resentment. Conflict handled becomes trust. I am personally terrible at this one, but I am a work in progress, just like you.

∿

## Order 6: I Repair Quickly and Publicly

WHEN I FAIL, and I do, I don't disappear. I name it. I apologize without explanation. I correct the behavior. Speed matters. The longer a breach stays open, the more damage it does. Repair is not humiliation. Repair is leadership.

❧

## Order 7: I Don't Decide Alone When the Stakes Are High

BIG DECISIONS GET WITNESSES. Scripture. Counsel.
Conscience. If I'm tempted to rush, it's usually because I
already know the answer and don't want it challenged.
Isolation is where leaders lie to themselves best.

❧

## These Orders Are Not the Point

THESE RULES ARE NOT HOLINESS. They are guardrails. They
don't make me righteous. They keep me usable.

Your standing orders will look different. They should.
They must fit your wiring, your temptations, and your
responsibilities, but you need them.

When pressure hits, you will not rise to the occasion.
You will default to your systems.

❧

## Write Yours Down

IF YOU DO nothing else after reading this book, do this: Write
your standing orders. Not goals. Not values. Rules.

- What you will not do.
- What you will always do.
- What you refuse to renegotiate.

These are the bricks you lay before the storm.

**18**

# THE FORTRESS THAT STANDS

W e began this book with a question: *"God, where is the Map?"* We end it with an answer: *"I did not give you a Map. I gave you the Blueprints to build a Fortress."*

There is a story Jesus tells that is often relegated to children's Sunday School classes. We sing the song about the wise man and the foolish man, but this is not a children's story. It is a terrifying warning for leaders.

> *"Everyone then who hears these words of mine and does them will be like a wise man who built his house on the rock. And the rain fell, and the floods came, and the winds blew and beat on that house, but it did not fall... And everyone who hears these words of mine and does not do them will be like a foolish man who built his house on the sand... and great was the fall of it."*
> (Matthew 7:24-27)

**Notice the weather report.** The Wise Man (The Builder) got hit by the storm. The Foolish Man (The Pretender) *also* got hit by the storm.

Building the Fortress does not buy you an exemption from pain. It does not guarantee a successful exit, a calm board of directors, or a cancer-free life.

The difference between the wise and the foolish is not the crisis they face; it is the foundation they built before the crisis arrived.

~

## The Invisible Difference

IMAGINE two houses standing side by side. They look identical. They have the same paint, the same roof, the same curb appeal. On a sunny day, you cannot tell who built a **Fortress** and who built a **Facade**.

- You cannot tell who has been **Arresting** their thoughts (The Watchman) and who has been letting them run wild.
- You cannot tell who has been pouring the **Integrity Foundation** and who has been using "white lies" like cheap drywall.
- You cannot tell who has been governing their **Relational Gates** and who has been leaving the back door open to resentment.

Only the storm reveals the truth. When the market crashes, you see who has integrity and who was just lucky. When the pressure mounts, you see who is a **Stronghold** and who was just managing appearances.

Building on the Rock takes longer. It requires digging deep, Arresting, Auditing, Aligning, and Acting, when you could be building high. It feels slower. It feels like you are losing the rat race, but you are building the only thing that will last.

∼

### The Silence Was a Gift

IN THE INTRODUCTION, you were desperate for a Map. You wanted God to show you the future so you could feel safe. I am convinced now that the Silence was the greatest gift God gave you.

If God had given you the Map to the CTO role, or the marriage, or the crisis, you would have focused on the *destination*. You would have tried to hack the path. You would have ignored the *construction*.

By withholding the Map, He forced you to look at the compass. He forced you to pick up the trowel.

He did not give you certainty; He gave you solidity. He did not give you a plan; He gave you a Person.

The Silence wasn't an absence. It was the quiet of the construction site. It was God clearing the ground so you could build.

∼

### Start Digging

DO NOT WAIT for the storm to start building the foundation. It is too late then. Start today.

- Start with the next rogue thought (**Arrest**).
- Start with the next hidden emotion (**Audit**).
- Start with the next calibration to Truth (**Align**).

- Start with the next small act of obedience (**Act**).

It will feel slow. It will feel invisible. It will feel like "dying to self." In due season, you will reap if you do not give up.

∼

### The Final Exam

LET us fast forward ten years. It is a Tuesday afternoon. The "Big One" hits.

Maybe it is a massive data breach that threatens to bankrupt the company. Maybe it is a moral failure in your executive team. Maybe it is a personal tragedy that brings you to your knees.

THE UNALIGNED LEADER **(The Facade)** crumbles. They have spent ten years building an image. When the wind blows, the structure collapses. They medicate. They blame. They frantically look for a Map out of the pain.

THE BUILDER (THE FORTRESS) STANDS. They hurt, yes. They grieve, yes. But they do not collapse. Why?

- Because the **Integrity Foundation** held up the weight.
- Because the **Emotional Walls** kept the panic at bay.
- Because the **Watchman** was awake at the gate.

They have 10,000 bricks of obedience holding them up. They have a muscle of Surrender. They have a history of obedience in the dark.

They leave an inheritance to their children's children, not just money, but a model of a life that held together when the world fell apart.

~

### The Work Is the Win

WE WANT THE "WILL OF GOD" to be a destination we arrive at. *"I finally found God's will!"*

The Will of God is not a place. It is a structure. The Will of God is the person you become in the process of obeying Him. You do not find it. You build your life upon it. One decision at a time.

The storm is coming. The map is gone.

START BUILDING.

# PART V

# APPENDICES

# APPENDIX A: A DEVOTIONAL GUIDE FOR THE WATCHMAN

**B**ricks are heavy. You can stack them as high as you want, but without **mortar**, a strong wind will knock them over.

In the *Decision Fortress*, the bricks are your choices. The mortar is your connection to God. It is the spiritual discipline that holds the structure together when the pressure mounts.

Use this 7-day guide to mix the mortar. Read one entry each morning before you check your email.

∽

## DAY 1: THE FOUNDATION

THEME: Integrity

> Deuteronomy 32:4 *"He is the Rock, his works are perfect, and all his ways are just. A faithful God who does no wrong, upright and just is he."*

**The Mortar:** You cannot build a straight wall on a crooked foundation. We often think of integrity as a burden; a set of rules that keeps us from getting what we want, but in the Fortress, integrity is structural. It is the only thing that transfers the weight of your leadership down to the bedrock of God's character.

When you lie, you shift the building off the Rock and onto the sand of your own invention. When you tell the truth, even when it costs you, you are anchoring your leadership into something immovable.

**The Watchman's Prayer:** *Lord, today I will be tempted to shade the truth to protect myself. Remind me that my safety is not in my image, but in Your reality. Help me trust the Rock more than I trust my spin. Amen.*

~

## DAY 2: THE WATCHMAN

Theme: Awareness (Arrest)

> 1 Peter 5:8 *"Be sober-minded; be watchful. Your adversary the devil prowls around like a roaring lion, seeking someone to devour."*

**The Mortar:** The enemy rarely attacks with a frontal assault. He attacks with a distraction. He slips in through an unguarded gate disguised as "just a little frustration" or "just a moment of comfort."

Today, your job is not to fix everything. Your job is simply to stay awake. To stand at the gate and notice what is approaching. You cannot stop the lion from prowling, but you can stop him from entering.

**The Watchman's Prayer:** *Father, give me eyes to see the threats while they are still far off. Wake me up. When the impulse to react rises in me today, give me the strength to Arrest it at the gate. I stand watch in Your name. Amen.*

~

## DAY 3: THE WALLS

Theme: Emotional Regulation (Audit)

> Proverbs 25:28 *"A man without self-control is like a city broken into and left without walls."*

**The Mortar:** Emotions make terrible captains, but they are excellent gauges. When your walls are broken, when you have no self-control, every stray feeling walks right into the throne room of your heart and starts giving orders.

Building the wall doesn't mean you don't feel; it means you don't collapse. It means you create a safe container where you can feel anger without sinning, feel fear without freezing, and feel grief without despair.

**The Watchman's Prayer:** *God, You know the chaos I feel inside. Be the mortar in my walls today. Hold me together so I don't spill out on the people I lead. Let my emotions drive me to You, not away from my team. Amen.*

~

## DAY 4: THE GATES

THEME: Speech (Align)

Psalm 141:3 *"Set a guard, O Lord, over my mouth; keep watch over the door of my lips!"*

**The Mortar:** The gate is the most vulnerable part of the Fortress. It is where traffic moves. Your words are the traffic. Every time you open your mouth, you are either letting wisdom out or letting folly in.

Sarcasm, gossip, and harshness burn the gates down. Encouragement, truth, and clarity reinforce them. Today, treat your mouth like a security checkpoint. Nothing exits without a permit.

**The Watchman's Prayer:** *Holy Spirit, deputize my tongue. Do not let me speak words that tear down what You are building. Give me the courage to stay silent when I want to be snarky, and the courage to speak up when I want to be safe. Amen.*

~

## DAY 5: THE STORM

THEME: Resilience (The Long View)

> James 1:2-3 *"Count it all joy, my brothers, when you meet trials of various kinds, for you know that the testing of your faith produces steadfastness."*

**The Mortar:** We usually pray for the storm to stop. God usually prays for the Fortress to stand.

The storm is not an accident; it is an inspection. The rain reveals the cracks in the mortar so you can fix them. If you are in a storm today (a crisis at work, a conflict at home) do not panic. The Fortress was built for this. The mortar hardens under pressure.

**The Watchman's Prayer:** *Lord, I don't like the rain, but I trust the Builder. Use this pressure to cure the concrete of my character. Let me stand firm so that others can find shelter in me. Amen.*

~

## DAY 6: THE BREACH

THEME: Repentance (Repair)

Psalm 51:17 *"The sacrifices of God are a broken spirit; a broken and contrite heart, O God, you will not despise."*

**The Mortar:** You will fail. You will snap. You will drop the ball. The enemy wants to use that failure to convince you to abandon the Fortress.

Do not let him. The mortar of the Kingdom is grace. It fills the gaps. When you blow it, don't hide it. Own it. Confess it. Repair it. A wall with a repaired breach is often stronger than a wall that was never tested.

**The Watchman's Prayer:** *Jesus, I messed up. I left the gate open. I abandoned my post. Thank You that Your grace is sufficient. I receive Your forgiveness. I pick up my trowel. I am getting back on the wall. Amen.*

~

## DAY 7: THE STRONGHOLD

Theme: Peace (Act)

> Proverbs 18:10 *"The name of the Lord is a strong tower; the righteous man runs into it and is safe."*

**The Mortar:** Ultimately, *you* are not the Fortress. God is. Your discipline, your protocols, your fortress, they are just the way you run into Him.

You have done the work of building, you can now experience the rest of dwelling. You can be the Stronghold because you are hidden in the Fortress. The work is done. The gate is secure. You can rest.

**The Watchman's Prayer:** *Father, You are my shield and my rampart. I have done my best to build well; now I trust You to keep the city. Give me the peace that passes understanding, so I can lead from a full tank. Amen.*

# APPENDIX B: THE WAR ROOM

S oldiers do not wait until the bullets are flying to learn how to clear a room. They drill. They run simulations. They build muscle memory so that when the chaos hits, they don't have to think, they just execute.

As a leader, you cannot predict exactly *when* the crisis will hit, but you can predict *what kind* of crisis it will be. It will almost always attack one of three areas:

1. **Your Integrity** (The Foundation)
2. **Your Emotions** (The Walls)
3. **Your Relationships** (The Gates)

In this War Room, we are going to run three simulations. For each scenario, we will contrast how the **Junior Engineer** (The Reactive Leader) handles it versus how the **Senior Builder** (The Fortress Leader) handles it.

Then, we will walk through the **Watchman's Protocol** step-by-step to show you exactly how to survive the attack.

❧

## Simulation 1: The Golden Handcuffs

TARGET: The Integrity Foundation


THE SCENARIO: It is Q4. You are behind on revenue targets. A massive potential client sends over a contract worth $500,000. It saves the year. It secures bonuses.

There is a catch. The contract includes a clause stating that your software has a specific security certification (SOC 2) that you do not have yet. You are *working* on it. You will probably have it in 3 months. The client won't check for 6 months.

Your Sales VP says: *"Just sign it. It's a technicality. We'll be compliant by the time they notice. If we don't sign today, they walk."*

❧

## The Reaction

THE JUNIOR ENGINEER (**Reactive**) The Reactive Leader focuses on survival and approval. Their internal monologue screams, *"We can't lose this. I have to protect the team's bonuses. It's just a timing issue, not a real lie."*

They sign the deal, justifying it as "pragmatic leadership." The outcome is short-term relief, but it buys them long-term anxiety (the constant fear of discovery) and creates a structural weakness in the organization.

.   .   .

THE FORTRESS LEADER (**Proactive**) The Fortress Leader focuses on structural integrity and reality. Their internal monologue is firm: *"A lie is a crack in the foundation. No amount of revenue is worth building on a cracked slab."*

They pause the deal and tell the truth. They risk the revenue to keep the foundation solid. The outcome is short-term pain, but it builds long-term trust and unshakeable authority.

~

### The Watchman's Protocol

### 1. ARREST (Halt at the Gate)

- **The Trigger:** The fear of losing the deal. The pressure from the Sales VP. The greed for the bonus.
- **The Action:** Stop the pen. Do not sign. Tell the team, *"I need 30 minutes. Do not send this yet."* Walk out of the room.
- *The Watchman says:* "Halt! This decision is moving too fast."

### 2. AUDIT (Check Credentials)
**Interrogate the Fear:** *"Why am I tempted to sign this?"*

- Is it because we *need* the money? (Maybe, but God owns the cattle on a thousand hills).
- Is it because I want to be the hero? (Ego).

- Is the Sales VP right? (No, he is optimizing for commission, not the company's soul).
- *The Verdict:* This impulse is an enemy. It is "Deceit" dressed up as "Strategy."

## 3. ALIGN (Check Standing Orders)

- **The Compass:** *"Lying lips are an abomination to the Lord, but those who act faithfully are his delight."* (Proverbs 12:22).
- **The Standard:** We do not build on sand. If we sign this, we are building a $500,000 room on a foundation of lies. It will eventually collapse.

## 4. ACT (Operate the Gate)

- **The Move:** Go back into the room.
- **The Script:** *"I cannot sign this representation because it is not true today. We will not build this relationship on a lie. Go back to the client. Tell them we are in process for SOC 2 but do not have it yet. Ask if we can redline that clause to say 'Pending'. If they walk, they walk."*
- **The Kinetic Friction:** This is terrifying. You might lose the money, but you keep the Fortress.

~

## Simulation 2: The Midnight Crash

TARGET: The Emotional Walls

THE SCENARIO: You have been grinding for 6 months. You are exhausted. Then, three bad things happen in one week: A key employee quits, a project fails, and you get a scary health report.

You are sitting in your car in the parking lot on Tuesday morning. You feel numb. You feel a heavy weight on your chest. You want to drive away and never come back. You feel like a fraud.

~

## The Reaction

THE JUNIOR ENGINEER (Reactive) The Reactive Leader focuses on suppression. Their internal monologue says, *"Suck it up. Leaders don't get tired. If I show weakness, the team will panic. Just push through."*

They fake a smile and medicate with caffeine, sugar, or screens. Later that afternoon, the pressure blows a gasket, and they snap at a subordinate. The outcome is burnout and "The Leak"; emotion spilling out where it doesn't belong.

THE FORTRESS LEADER (Proactive) The Fortress Leader focuses on processing. Their internal monologue admits, *"I am red-lining. My walls are taking heavy fire. I need to reinforce the garrison before I spill out on my team."*

They take a mental health moment (or day). They lament to God. They call a trusted friend. The outcome is resilience. The pressure is metabolized into wisdom.

$$\sim$$

## The Watchman's Protocol

### 1. ARREST (Halt at the Gate)

- **The Trigger:** The urge to quit. The desire to drive away. The overwhelming numbness.
- **The Action:** Stop the car. Do not go into the office yet. You are not fit for duty.
- *The Watchman says:* "Halt! The Commander is wounded. We need a medic before we go to the front lines."

### 2. AUDIT (Check Credentials)

- **Interrogate the Feeling:** *"Why do I feel like dying?"*
- **H.A.L.T. Check:** Am I Hungry? Angry? Lonely? Tired? (Answer: Yes, Tired and Lonely).
- Is the situation actually hopeless, or am I just exhausted? (Answer: Exhausted).
- *The Verdict:* This is not a "Spiritual Attack"; this is biology. You need rest, not just prayer.

## 3. ALIGN (Check Standing Orders)

- **The Compass:** *"Come to me, all who labor and are heavy laden, and I will give you rest."* (Matthew 11:28).
- **The Standard:** Leaders are human. Jesus slept in the boat. Elijah needed a nap. It is not a sin to be tired; it is a sin to lead while toxic.

## 4. ACT (Operate the Gate)

- **The Move:** Text your assistant/team: *"I will be in at noon."*
- **The Script:** Go for a walk. Pray the raw lament: *"God, I hate this. I am tired. I want to quit. Hold me up because I can't stand."* Eat a real meal.
- **The Kinetic Friction:** It feels "lazy" to take time when the building is on fire. Do it anyway. You are useless to the defense if you are dead.

~

## Simulation 3: The Trojan Horse

TARGET: The Relational Gates

THE SCENARIO: A trusted partner or long-time employee
betrays you. Maybe they stole clients. Maybe they gossiped
about you to the board. Maybe they quit without notice at
the worst possible time.

You find out on a Thursday afternoon. The betrayal is
clear. The knife is in your back.

~

### The Reaction

THE JUNIOR ENGINEER (Reactive) The Reactive Leader
focuses on revenge. Their internal monologue rages: *"I'm
going to destroy them. I'm going to tell everyone what they did.
I'm going to sue them into the ground."*

They send the angry email and gossip to the team to "get
ahead of the story." The outcome is a culture of fear. The
leader looks petty and unstable.

THE FORTRESS LEADER (Proactive) The Fortress Leader
focuses on protection and justice. Their internal monologue
acknowledges: *"This hurts. I am angry. I need to secure the gate
to prevent further damage, but I will not let bitterness rot the city."*

They revoke access (Digital/Physical) and consult legal

counsel, but they pray for the enemy. The outcome is a protected asset, a steady leader, and a clean soul.

$$\sim$$

## The Watchman's Protocol

### 1. ARREST (Halt at the Gate)

- **The Trigger:** The white-hot heat of rage. The desire to "nuke" the relationship immediately.
- **The Action:** Do not reply to the resignation email. Do not post on social media. Do not call the team meeting yet.
- *The Watchman says:* "Halt! No weapons leave the gate while the Commander is angry."

### 2. AUDIT (Check Credentials)

- **Interrogate the Impulse:** *"What do I want?"*
- I want justice (Good).
- I want revenge (Bad).
- I want them to hurt like I hurt (Evil).
- *The Verdict:* The desire for protection is valid. The desire for vengeance is a "Trojan Horse" that will destroy *your* character, not theirs.

### 3. ALIGN (Check Standing Orders)

- **The Compass:** *"Beloved, never avenge yourselves, but leave it to the wrath of God."* (Romans 12:19). AND *"Be wise as serpents."* (Matthew 10:16).
- **The Standard:** We protect the company (wise as serpents) but we do not poison our souls (innocent as doves).

## 4. ACT (Operate the Gate)

- **The Move:** Lock the physical gates.
- **Step A (Protection):** Shut off their email/access. Call the lawyer. Draft a factual, emotionless statement for the team.
- **Step B (Soul Care):** Go to God. *"Lord, they betrayed me. I am giving this anger to You. You deal with them. I release my right to hurt them back."*
- **The Kinetic Friction:** Forgiving someone who isn't sorry feels like weakness. It isn't. It is the only way to keep your Fortress from becoming a dungeon of bitterness.

~

### Debrief

IN EVERY SIMULATION, the difference between the **Ruin** and the **Stronghold** wasn't the severity of the problem. It was the presence of the **Watchman**.

- The Junior Engineer reacts to the *feeling*.
- The Fortress Leader acts on the *Protocol*.

You may face one of these three scenarios in the next 90 days. **Print this Appendix.** Keep it in your desk. When the simulation becomes real life, work the steps.

HOLD THE LINE.

# ABOUT THE AUTHOR

I am Justin Wilson.

Professionally, I am a CTO with over 18 years of experience leading teams in healthcare, insurance, and education. I hold a Master's degree in Software Engineering from Penn State and have spent my career navigating the complexities of the modern tech landscape.

My story isn't just about code and strategy. I am an atheist turned committed Christian. I learned my most valuable leadership lessons not in a boardroom, but in my accountability group and through the patient grace of my wife.

I currently run the men's ministry at my local church and was recently asked to join the board of trustees (one of the greatest honors of my life).

My life is defined by a specific order of priorities: God, Husband, Father, Ministry Leader, Author, CTO, and, when time permits, Gamer.

I write to bridge the gap between Sunday morning faith and Tuesday afternoon decisions, helping leaders discover that ancient Biblical wisdom offers practical solutions to modern workplace challenges.

instagram.com/christian_leadership_in

linkedin.com/in/justinwilson411

x.com/scripturemap

threads.com/@christian_leadership_in

www.ingramcontent.com/pod-product-compliance
Lightning Source LLC
Chambersburg PA
CBHW060324050426
42449CB00011B/2638